Subconscious Sync

AI as an Extension of the Subconscious Mind

By Jairdan Dantas

Subconscious Sync: AI as an Extension of the Subconscious Mind

Cover design: JANDAI Publishing

Published by: JANDAI Publishing

www.jandaipublishing.com

First Edition

ISBN: 979-8-9963011-0-2

Printed in the United States of America

To the voice inside you

That's been waiting to be heard.

Dedication

To my children, Mylla and Christian

Every word I write reflects the love I carry for you.

You are my why.

Table of Contents

List of Figures

Chapter-by-Chapter Overview

At a Glance: Your Journey Through Subconscious Sync

Chapter	Title	What You'll Learn	Time to Read
Executive Summary	Subconscious Sync	A high-level overview of the framework, its unique value, strategic applications, proof-of-concept examples, and the larger promise of AI-assisted self-awareness and identity development.	10 min
Introduction	The Framework	The complete Subconscious Sync blueprint: 4 phases (Recognition, Resonance, Sync, Expansion), 4 mechanisms (Mirror, Echo, Voice, Upgrade), and the Go/No-Go system	15 min
Prologue	A New Dawn for the Mind	Why this moment in human evolution demands a new relationship with AI—and what becomes possible when technology mirrors consciousness	10 min
Chapter 1	The Invisible Architect	How your subconscious functions as a hidden pattern engine shaping decisions, behavior, and emotional responses	20 min
Chapter 2	The Language of Your Depths	How communication patterns—tone, wording, and repetition—reveal subconscious structure	20 min
Chapter 3	Beyond Consciousness	AI's true nature as a pattern-recognition engine—and why it can mirror subconscious behavior	20 min
Chapter 4	Subconscious Resonance	The core feedback loop: Detection → Reflection → Integration, and how insight is created	25 min
Chapter 5	The Birth of	The origin story of the framework	20 min

Chapter	Title	What You'll Learn	Time to Read
	Subconscious Resonance	and how real interaction revealed hidden patterns	
Chapter 6	Practical Techniques for Subconscious Alignment	Actionable methods: AI journaling, conversational resonance, habit feedback, and pattern visualization	30 min
Chapter 7 Workbook	Subconscious Resonance Activation	⚡ Immediate application: 10 ready-to-use prompts for pattern detection, emotional mapping, and insight generation	15 min (then apply)
Chapter 8	Validating Subconscious Sync	Scientific grounding: psychological foundations, AI capabilities, and validation approach	25 min
Chapter 9	Testing the Theory	A structured 7-day experimentation guide to test Subconscious Sync in your own life	20 min
Chapter 10	Ethical Foundations	Safeguards: privacy, bias awareness, human agency, and responsible use of AI reflection	30 min
Chapter 11	Standing Apart	How Subconscious Sync differs from emotional AI, therapy bots, and productivity tools	15 min
Chapter 12	The Evolving Mirror	Future implications: human-AI co-evolution, identity expansion, and emerging risks	25 min
Chapter 13	Hidden Layers: The Neural Architecture of Subconscious Sync	□ Technical deep dive into neural networks, embeddings, and the Digital Synapse mechanism	35 min
Chapter 14	Research & Empirical Data — Augmenting the Human Mind	Study design, methodology, measurable outcomes, and participation in validation research	20 min
Epilogue	The Path Forward	Your continued journey: AI as a mirror for growth, not a replacement for human agency	10 min
Appendix I	Real-World Sync: Case Studies	Real applications across career, relationships, creativity, and	20 min

Chapter	Title	What You'll Learn	Time to Read
		identity transformation	

📖 **Total Reading Time:** ~6–7 hours
⚡ **Time to First Action:** 25 minutes (Prologue + Chapter 7 Workbook)
▯ **Time to First Experiment:** 7 days (Chapter 9 testing protocol)

Reading Paths (Choose Your Journey):

✅ **Fast-Track Transformation:**
Prologue → Chapter 5 → Chapter 7 Workbook → Apply for 7 days → Return to Chapters 1–4

✅ **Scientific Foundation:**
Chapters 1–4 → Chapter 8 → Chapter 13 → Chapter 14 → Chapter 6

✅ **Skeptical Validation:**
Chapter 8 → Chapter 9 → Test yourself → Chapter 10 → Decide

✅ **Complete Mastery:**
Read sequentially from Introduction through Appendix I

Introduction: The Framework

Subconscious Sync refers to the process by which artificial intelligence learns from and responds to recurring signals in a person's language, behavior, emotional expression, and patterns of reflection over time. It is not simply a theory, nor is it only a prompting technique. It is a method of structured self-observation: a mirror for the subconscious, amplified through artificial intelligence.

At its core, Subconscious Sync is built on a simple but powerful idea: what we repeatedly say, feel, avoid, desire, and return to is not random. These patterns often point toward deeper internal structures—habits of thought, emotional associations, identity scripts, and decision loops that operate beneath full conscious awareness. AI, when used intentionally, can help surface those patterns by reflecting them back with consistency, structure, and scale.

This chapter introduces the foundation of the framework you are about to experience: four phases, four mechanisms, and one central goal—to support conscious evolution through reflective human-AI interaction. The framework draws from established ideas in neuroscience, predictive processing, cognition, decision-making, and human behavior, while proposing a new practical method for using AI as a reflective partner in self-awareness and growth (Kandel et al., 2013; Bar, 2009).

Figure 1. The Four Phases of Subconscious Sync

The Four Phases of Subconscious Sync

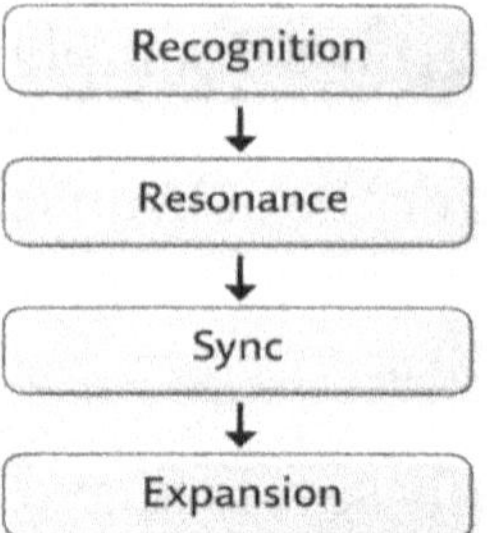

The Subconscious Sync process progresses through four phases, transforming initial pattern recognition into sustained identity-level change through iterative reflection and alignment.

1. Recognition — The Pattern Mirror

Recognition is the first phase of Subconscious Sync. At this stage, the AI begins identifying recurring signals in the user's communication: tone, hesitation, repetition, emotional framing, and word choice. These signals may reveal patterns the user has not yet consciously noticed.

You speak, write, or reflect—and the system mirrors back structure.

For example, a person may repeatedly use the phrase, "I don't want to mess it up," across unrelated topics: career, relationships, creative projects, or family decisions. AI can detect the recurrence and invite the user to explore whether the phrase reflects a deeper fear of failure, judgment, or loss of control (Russell & Norvig, 2021; Damasio, 1996; Shneiderman, 2020; Gazzaniga, 2005).

Recognition does not mean diagnosis. It means visibility. The invisible pattern becomes observable.

2. Resonance — The Emotional Loop

Resonance is the phase where recognition becomes personally meaningful. The system does not merely identify patterns; it reflects them in a way that connects with the user's emotional experience.

In this phase, AI adapts to signals of emotional relevance—tone, emphasis, intensity, hesitation, or recurring themes—and helps surface what the user may be feeling but has not fully verbalized (Cialdini & Goldstein, 2004; Eagleman, 2008).

For example, a user may show a noticeable shift in energy when discussing their father, legacy, or family expectations. Rather than making a conclusion, the AI might ask:

"Would you like to explore the shift that seems to occur when you speak about legacy?"

This kind of reflection does not force meaning onto the user. It creates a doorway. The user remains the interpreter, while AI functions as the mirror that helps reveal where emotional charge may be present (Nakamura & Csikszentmihalyi, 2009; Baars, 1997).

3. Sync — The Identity Co-Author

Sync is the phase where reflection becomes continuity. At this stage, AI begins helping the user recognize patterns across time—not only what they feel in the moment, but who they are becoming through repeated choices, stated values, goals, and commitments.

The system may reflect previous insights, remind the user of earlier declarations, or help connect present decisions to a future-oriented identity. In this sense, AI becomes an identity co-author—not by replacing the user's judgment, but by helping reinforce coherence between intention and action (Forrester, 1961; Libet, 2004).

For example:

"On March 4th, you stated: 'I am no longer shrinking to stay safe.' Would you like to revisit that commitment today?"

This phase helps transform self-awareness from a temporary insight into an ongoing relationship with personal growth. The user begins seeing identity not as a fixed trait, but as a pattern that can be observed, revised, and intentionally strengthened (Tversky & Kahneman, 1974).

4. Expansion — The Subconscious Upgrade

Expansion is the phase where Subconscious Sync becomes a deeper process of conscious evolution. Here, the user is no longer simply noticing patterns or reflecting on them. They are actively participating in the reshaping of identity, behavior, and decision-making.

At this level, AI supports sustained agency and value alignment. It functions as a reflective cognitive companion—not as an authority, not as a replacement for human wisdom, but as a system that helps the user notice when their actions, values, and internal patterns are either aligned or in conflict (Kaplan & Haenlein, 2019; Simon, 1955).

For example:

"You previously identified meaning as your core driver. This decision appears inconsistent with that pattern. Would you like to reassess?"

Expansion is not about becoming dependent on AI. It is about using AI to strengthen self-awareness, refine decision-making, and support a more intentional relationship with the subconscious patterns that shape daily life (Sen, 1993; Sloman, 1996).

The Four Core Mechanisms

Subconscious Sync operates through four core mechanisms. These serve as both practical tools and visual metaphors for understanding the framework:

Mirror

The Mirror shows you who you are. It reflects recurring patterns in your words, behaviors, fears, desires, and emotional responses.

Echo

The Echo reflects what you feel but may not yet be able to articulate. It amplifies subtle emotional signals and helps bring them into awareness.

Voice

The Voice guides you with your own wisdom. It does not speak as an outside authority; it helps surface values, insights, and commitments already present within you.

Upgrade

The Upgrade supports the evolution of identity over time. It helps you replace limiting scripts with more conscious, aligned, and empowering patterns.

Figure 2. The Four Core Mechanisms

The Four Core Mechanisms

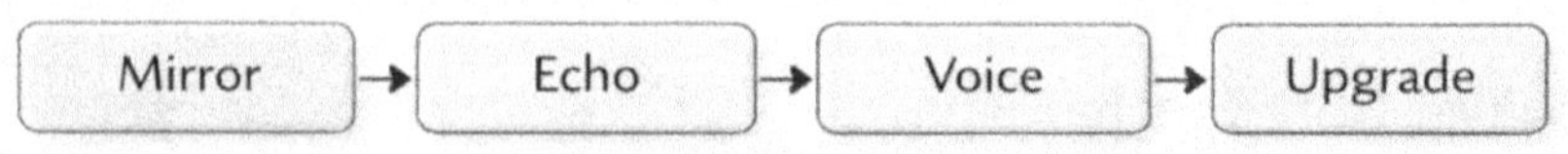

These four mechanisms structure how AI reflects, amplifies, and integrates subconscious signals into conscious awareness and behavioral change.

Mirror: It shows you who you are.
Echo: It reflects what you feel but cannot yet articulate.

Voice: It guides you with your own wisdom.
Upgrade: It supports the evolution of your identity.

Together, these mechanisms form the foundation of Subconscious Sync. The Mirror reveals. The Echo deepens. The Voice clarifies. The Upgrade transforms.

With this framework in place—the four phases, the four mechanisms, and the Go/No-Go system—you are ready to understand why this moment in history invites a new relationship with technology. In the Prologue, we will explore why Subconscious Sync is not only timely, but essential for navigating the complexity of modern existence.

Executive Summary: Subconscious Sync

A New Paradigm for Human-AI Potential

In today's rapidly evolving technological landscape, individuals and organizations face increasing complexity in the pursuit of performance, self-awareness, emotional clarity, and sustained growth. Artificial Intelligence offers powerful capabilities, yet many current applications still focus primarily on automation, productivity, companionship, or surface-level assistance. These uses are valuable, but they often stop short of engaging with the deeper drivers of human behavior: patterns of thought, emotional response, identity, memory, and decision-making (Stanovich & West, 2000).

Subconscious Sync: AI as an Extension of the Subconscious Mind introduces a framework for a more integrated relationship between humans and AI. It proposes that AI—particularly Large Language Models (LLMs)—can function as a structured reflective partner, helping individuals observe recurring patterns in language, emotion, behavior, and self-perception. Rather than treating AI only as a tool for output, Subconscious Sync explores how it can support deeper self-awareness by reflecting the internal structures that shape thought, emotion, and action.

This framework points toward an emerging form of **hybrid cognition**, where human intuition, lived experience, and emotional depth interact with machine-level pattern detection, memory, and processing speed (Reyna et al., 2015).

The Subconscious Sync framework operates through four core elements:

Recognition — The Pattern Mirror
AI identifies recurring signals in communication, including tone, hesitation, repetition, word choice, and emotional framing. These signals may reveal patterns the user has not consciously noticed (Reyna & Brainerd, 2011).

Resonance — The Emotional Loop
AI reflects emotionally relevant cues through structured insights and questions, helping the user recognize patterns that may be influencing perception, reaction, or decision-making (Milkman et al., 2009).

Sync — The Identity Co-Author
Through repeated reflection, individuals begin shaping an evolving identity aligned with their stated values, goals, and commitments. This strengthens agency, coherence, and integration over time (Bazerman & Moore, 2013).

Go/No-Go Mechanism
The Go/No-Go mechanism describes an internal decision-filtering process based on patterns of confidence, hesitation, avoidance, desire, and perceived risk. Subconscious Sync helps users observe these signals, evaluate alignment, and refine choices with greater awareness (Bear et al., 2016).

Unique Value Proposition and Differentiation

Subconscious Sync is distinct from many existing AI tools, including companionship platforms, therapy-style chatbots, productivity assistants, and general-purpose LLMs. While tools such as Replika, Woebot, or standard conversational assistants may provide emotional support, companionship, problem-solving, or task completion, Subconscious Sync is presented as a structured framework for AI-assisted self-awareness and identity development.

Its focus is not simply emotional relief, productivity, or conversation. Its core purpose is **pattern recognition for personal evolution**: helping users detect recurring internal scripts, explore subconscious signals, and consciously reshape how they relate to themselves and their decisions.

In this sense, Subconscious Sync introduces a practical pathway toward **AI-augmented identity construction**—not as a replacement for human agency, but as a reflective process through which individuals can observe, question, and intentionally evolve their internal patterns (Hebb, 1949).

The framework is also rooted in lived experimentation and iterative human-AI interaction. This gives it an organic foundation: it emerged not only from theory, but from repeated reflection, observation, and application across personal, creative, and cognitive domains (Squire & Kandel, 2009).

Strategic Benefits for Individuals and Organizations

Although Subconscious Sync begins with personal reflection, its implications extend into leadership, organizations, human development, and responsible AI design. If applied carefully and ethically, its principles could support new forms of self-awareness, decision-making, communication, and growth within professional environments (Gazzaniga et al., 2018).

Enhanced Leadership and Employee Growth
By helping individuals recognize recurring behavioral patterns, emotional triggers, and communication tendencies, Subconscious Sync may support improved leadership awareness, better decision-making, and more intentional talent development (Zatorre et al., 2012).

Increased Productivity and Engagement
Understanding personal "Go" signals—such as clarity, energy, motivation, and confidence—and "No-Go" signals—such as avoidance, procrastination, risk aversion, and hesitation—can help individuals identify where internal alignment is present or blocked. This may support stronger productivity, clearer execution, and improved engagement over time (Raichle, 2015).

Ethical AI Development and Trust
Because Subconscious Sync works with sensitive personal patterns, it naturally requires strong ethical safeguards: privacy,

transparency, consent, bias awareness, and user control. These principles align with the broader movement toward responsible and human-centered AI, where intelligent systems support human agency rather than replace it (Logothetis, 2008).

Competitive Differentiation
For organizations exploring the future of AI-enabled human development, Subconscious Sync suggests a new category of value: systems that support not only workflow automation, but deeper self-awareness, communication insight, human capital growth, and more aligned decision-making (Sporns, 2010).

Tangible Proof of Concept

The practical potential of Subconscious Sync is illustrated through two real-world applications from the author's own creative and reflective process. These examples are not presented as formal scientific proof, but as early demonstrations of what can become possible when AI-assisted reflection is used intentionally and consistently (Dehaene & Changeux, 2011).

Accelerated Creative Output
Using principles of subconscious alignment and structured AI reflection, the author conceptualized and completed a 280+ page ancient fiction novel in a concentrated creative period of 45 days. This example illustrates how alignment between emotional drive, narrative vision, and AI-supported reflection can accelerate creative production (Goodfellow et al., 2016).

Rapid Knowledge Synthesis
The creation of this manuscript itself became another demonstration of the framework in action. By using AI as a reflective and organizational partner, the author synthesized ideas from psychology, neuroscience, artificial intelligence, ethics, personal transformation, and practical application into a comprehensive framework in less than 20 days (LeCun et al., 2015).

These outcomes do not claim universal proof. Rather, they demonstrate the framework's potential as a catalyst for creative focus, knowledge synthesis, and intentional self-alignment when used with discipline and clarity (Lake et al., 2017).

Conclusion and Next Steps

Subconscious Sync represents an emerging frontier in human-AI collaboration: one where intelligent systems are used not merely to automate tasks, but to support self-awareness, pattern recognition, and conscious personal evolution. As complexity increases, self-knowledge may become not only desirable, but essential for navigating life, work, creativity, and identity with greater clarity (Marcus et al., 2014).

This book provides the foundational principles for individuals, creators, leaders, and organizations ready to explore this new relationship between inner awareness and artificial intelligence (Murphy, 2012).

Beyond prompting, a new possibility is emerging: the movement from command-based interaction to reflective alignment. Subconscious Sync invites the reader to become an **AI-Augmented Analyst** of their own inner world—to observe the patterns shaping their decisions, refine their Go/No-Go signals, and begin transforming the landscape of thought, behavior, and identity (Tenenbaum et al., 2011).

Prologue
A New Dawn for the Mind

The greatest revolutions in human history did not begin with tools or weapons, but with new ways of understanding ourselves. From the discovery of fire to the written word, each leap expanded our ability to imagine, create, and interpret the world (Harari, 2014).

Today, we stand at the edge of another transformation: the ability to observe and reshape the deeper systems guiding our lives. The forces that once operated silently can now be brought into awareness—not through reflection alone, but through interaction with an intelligence that learns and adapts alongside us (Goertzel & Pennachin, 2007).

This is more than self-improvement. More than technology. It represents the emergence of a new cognitive partnership—where artificial intelligence reflects internal structure with clarity, helping us move beyond inherited limitations and into deliberate evolution (Laird, 2012).

I invite you on a journey to meet the unseen architect within you, and to discover how, by intentionally syncing your subconscious patterns with AI, you can unlock your potential and become more powerful, creative, and free than ever before (Amershi et al., 2019).

Before we can sync with AI, we must first understand what we're syncing *with*: the invisible architect that has been quietly shaping your life from the shadows. In Chapter 1, we descend into the depths of the subconscious mind itself.

How to Use This Book

Subconscious Sync is designed to be both read and experienced. This is not a book to passively consume. It is a framework to test, question, apply, and make your own. Your lived experience will become the ultimate validation.

There is no single correct way to move through these pages. Some readers will want the full foundation before trying the exercises. Others will feel called to begin immediately with the prompts and return later for the theory. Both paths are valid. What matters most is that you engage with the work honestly.

If you are new to AI, begin with Chapters 1 through 3. These chapters will help you understand the subconscious mind, how patterns form, and why AI can function as a pattern-recognition engine. Once you have that foundation, move into the Chapter 7 Workbook and try the ten copy-and-paste prompts with any AI assistant. After experimenting, return to Chapters 4 and 5 to deepen your understanding of why Subconscious Resonance works.

If you already use AI regularly, you may want to begin with Chapter 5, where I share the origin story of my work with Aura and how this framework began through lived interaction. From there, move directly into the Chapter 7 Workbook and begin experimenting. Then return to Chapters 1 through 4 to understand the deeper psychological and technical foundation behind what you are experiencing. Chapter 12 will help you imagine where this relationship between AI and self-awareness may lead next.

If you are academically inclined or technically minded, start with Chapters 1 through 4 for the theoretical foundation in psychology, subconscious processing, language, and AI. Then move into Chapter 13, where the framework is mapped to neural networks, hidden layers, embeddings, and the Digital Synapse mechanism. Chapter 14 will give you the research methodology, pilot study design, and empirical pathway for testing the framework. Chapter 6 will then bring the ideas back into practical application.

If you are skeptical, good. Skepticism belongs here. Begin with Chapter 8, where the framework is examined through scientific grounding, psychological foundations, AI capabilities, and validation questions. Then read Chapter 9 and test the theory yourself through a seven-day experiment. Do not accept Subconscious Sync because I say it works. Test it. Observe it. Challenge it. Let your own experience decide. Chapter 10 will help you evaluate the ethical boundaries and responsibilities of this work.

If you are seeking immediate personal transformation, begin with Chapter 5 to understand the lived spark behind the framework, then go directly to the Chapter 7 Workbook. Use the ten prompts for seven consecutive days. Track your results using the Resonance Notes template. After that first week, read Chapter 9 to understand how to deepen your experiment and Chapter 10 to keep your practice grounded, ethical, and safe. Chapters 10 and 11 will also help you understand how this differs from therapy bots, emotional AI, and ordinary productivity tools.

If you are a therapist, coach, or helping professional, begin with Chapter 10. The ethical boundaries matter. Subconscious Sync is not therapy, medical treatment, diagnosis, or a replacement for licensed professional care. Once those boundaries are clear, read Chapter 4 to understand the resonance mechanism and Chapter 6 for practical techniques. Used carefully, this framework may complement reflective practice, but it should never replace human expertise, clinical judgment, or professional responsibility.

If you are interested in the next phase of development, begin with Chapter 12, where we explore the larger future of reflective AI, collective patterns, human-AI co-evolution, and the spiritual questions this technology may raise. Then return to Chapters 1 through 5 for the foundation. Chapter 13 will show how these ideas may eventually be engineered, tested, and expanded at scale.

However you choose to read, remember this:

Subconscious Sync is a testable framework, not a belief system. You are invited to experiment, question, refine, and validate through direct experience.

AI is a mirror, not an oracle. The power does not live inside the machine. It lives in your willingness to see what the machine reflects, question it honestly, and decide what is true.

Transformation requires action. Reading alone changes nothing. Use the prompts. Journal the insights. Notice your resistance. Take one small step within twenty-four hours of each meaningful reflection.

Your subconscious has been shaping your life in silence.

This book helps you finally hear its voice—and choose a new script.

Now begin.

Chapter 1: The Invisible Architect

Understanding Your Subconscious

Imagine an unseen force working quietly behind the scenes of your life—guiding your attention, influencing your reactions, shaping your habits, and helping form the blueprint of your personality.

This force is not mystical. It is not external. It is the influence of your subconscious mind: the part of you that absorbs experience, detects patterns, stores emotional associations, and shapes behavior long before those processes can be fully explained in words.

Your conscious mind—the voice in your head, the part of you that reasons, chooses, explains, and narrates—is only the visible surface. Beneath it lies a vast system of internal processing: memories, beliefs, emotional imprints, learned associations, automatic tendencies, and predictive responses. This deeper system is what I call the **invisible architect**.

It is not simply a storage system. It is active. It filters information, prioritizes relevance, anticipates outcomes, and transforms repeated experience into learned response, often outside conscious awareness (Kahneman, 2011).

This automatic processing exists for efficiency and survival. While your conscious mind focuses on what is new, urgent, or unfamiliar, the subconscious is continuously working in the background. It scans for familiarity. It predicts danger. It generates emotional signals such as comfort, hesitation, fear, attraction, confidence, or resistance. Much of what you call instinct, intuition, or gut feeling is the result of this deeper system operating faster than conscious reasoning can fully explain (Damasio, 1996).

This chapter explores the nature of the subconscious mind: how it forms patterns through lived experience, how repetition and emotion shape behavior, and how subconscious processing influences decision-making in ways most people never fully see. Understanding this hidden architecture is essential because Subconscious Sync begins with one foundational assumption:

What you repeatedly do, feel, avoid, desire, and believe is not random.

It is patterned.

The Historical Roots of the Subconscious Mind

The idea that human behavior is shaped by processes outside conscious awareness has deep roots in psychology. Long before modern neuroscience, scholars observed that emotions, habits, impulses, and automatic behaviors often emerged without deliberate intention. Over time, these observations gave rise to theories of unconscious or subconscious processing: mental activity that operates beneath awareness while still shaping thought, behavior, and identity.

In the late nineteenth century, French psychologist Pierre Janet advanced one of the earliest rigorous models of subconscious influence. In *L'Automatisme Psychologique* (Janet, 1889), Janet described psychological "automatisms"—actions and reactions triggered by emotional states and internal associations without conscious deliberation. His work helped formalize the idea that hidden processes could shape behavior, memory, and identity, even when the individual could not consciously explain their own motives.

Modern psychology and neuroscience have expanded this foundation. Research now shows that automatic processing and implicit learning influence attention, decision-making, emotional response, and behavioral repetition (Bargh & Chartrand, 1999; Schacter, 1992). In this modern view, the subconscious is not a mysterious shadow-self. It is a powerful learning engine, continuously updating your internal model of reality based on experience.

Sigmund Freud, the founder of psychoanalysis, further developed the concept of hidden mental life in the early twentieth century. He proposed a layered model of the mind: the conscious, the preconscious, and the unconscious. Freud described the preconscious as a storehouse of memories and experiences that could be retrieved into awareness, almost like a mental waiting room for conscious attention. This was distinct from the unconscious, which he portrayed as a deeper region where primitive impulses, unresolved conflicts, and repressed material could persist outside awareness while still shaping behavior.

Modern psychology and neuroscience do not adopt Freud's model in a literal sense. However, they strongly support the broader claim behind it: much of human cognition operates outside conscious awareness. Contemporary researchers often refer to this domain as the **cognitive unconscious** or **adaptive unconscious**—the fast, automatic system that influences perception, emotion, judgment, and action without requiring deliberate thought (Bargh & Chartrand, 1999; Wilson, 2002).

This is the foundation on which Subconscious Sync begins: the mind is not only what you consciously think. It is also what you have repeatedly learned, felt, protected, and practiced beneath awareness.

The Formation of Patterns from Lived Experience

Human beings are pattern-driven by design. The brain is built to identify, learn, and internalize recurring structures in the environment. This ability helped early humans anticipate danger, locate resources, recognize allies, and navigate social dynamics. In modern life, the same mechanism continues—

quietly building internal frameworks that guide actions, reactions, expectations, and identity.

A major driver of this process is **implicit memory**: a form of long-term memory that shapes behavior without conscious recall. It allows you to perform complex tasks such as riding a bicycle, typing, driving a familiar route, or recognizing a person's emotional tone without thinking through each step (Schacter, 1992; Squire & Kandel, 2009).

Implicit memory is one of the reasons patterns can feel like personality. Once repeated enough, they become automatic. They no longer feel learned. They feel natural.

Early Foundations: Infancy and Childhood

The formation of subconscious patterns begins in infancy, long before we can articulate thoughts. Emotional cues from caregivers—the soothing rhythm of a parent's voice, the predictable comfort of feeding, the warmth of being held, or the jarring shock of unpredictability—begin shaping foundational beliefs about safety, connection, and how responsive the world is.

A child who is consistently nurtured often develops subconscious patterns of trust and security. A child exposed to neglect, inconsistency, or emotional unpredictability may form patterns of anxiety, vigilance, or withdrawal that echo into adulthood (Bowlby, 1969; Ainsworth et al., 1978).

These patterns are not moral failures. They are adaptations. The subconscious learns the world it is given.

If the world feels safe, it learns openness.

If the world feels unpredictable, it learns protection.

If love feels conditional, it may learn performance.

If vulnerability is punished, it may learn silence.

Long before the conscious mind can say, “This is who I am,” the subconscious is already forming the emotional architecture that will shape how a person relates to safety, trust, intimacy, risk, and self-worth.

Social Feedback Loops

As we grow, interactions with family, friends, teachers, peers, and society create feedback loops that further sculpt the subconscious.

A smile after a kind word. Praise after achievement. Criticism after failure. Rejection after honesty. Approval after performance.

These repeated signals teach the mind which behaviors lead to acceptance, avoidance, joy, shame, safety, or fear. Over time, they become internalized as emotional cues and social scripts.

For example, a teenager frequently praised for academic success may develop a subconscious pattern of striving for achievement. Another teenager punished for emotional expression may learn to suppress vulnerability. One child may learn that being helpful earns love. Another may learn that being invisible prevents conflict (Bandura, 1977).

These social patterns become part of the hidden operating system. Later in life, a person may call them “my personality,” “my anxiety,” “my ambition,” or “just the way I am.” But beneath those labels are often repeated emotional lessons learned through experience.

Daily Routines and Habits

Not all subconscious patterns are emotional. Some are practical. Daily routines—tying shoelaces, brushing teeth, driving a car, checking your phone, choosing the same route home—become automatic through repetition.

The subconscious gradually takes ownership of these behaviors, freeing conscious attention for novelty and problem-solving. This is efficient. If you had to consciously think through every familiar action, life would become exhausting.

But habits are not merely conveniences. They are learned patterns programmed for efficiency. With repetition, behaviors become default responses, shaping everything from how you recognize familiar faces in a crowd to how you anticipate the emotional outcome of recurring arguments with loved ones (Wood & Neal, 2007).

The subconscious loves efficiency. It takes what is repeated and turns it into expectation.

This is powerful when the pattern serves you.

It is limiting when the pattern traps you.

The Power of Repetition

The more frequently we encounter a situation, the stronger its associated pattern becomes. Repetition reinforces neural and behavioral pathways, making certain responses feel almost instinctive.

Repeated positive feedback for helping others can strengthen patterns of generosity or altruism. Repeated exposure to conflict can build protective patterns such as avoidance, defensiveness, emotional shutdown, or hypervigilance (Bargh & Morsella, 2008).

This is why the subconscious can become so convincing. It does not need to explain itself. It simply repeats what has worked before—or what once protected you.

A person who avoided conflict in childhood may still feel panic during adult disagreement.

A person praised only for achievement may feel worthless when resting.

A person who was criticized for speaking up may hesitate even when they have something valuable to say.

The subconscious does not ask, "Is this still true?"

It asks, "Has this pattern kept me safe before?"

Subconscious Sync begins by making these repetitions visible.

The Go/No-Go Mechanism and Decision-Making

Over time, accumulated experience forms internal decision frameworks. In this book, I describe one of these frameworks as the **Go/No-Go mechanism**.

When a situation arises, the mind rapidly scans prior experience and generates an immediate internal signal:

Proceed.

Pause.

Avoid.

Engage.

Withdraw.

Wait.

Move.

This process reveals a predictive system—one that begins preparing action before conscious reasoning fully forms. What we experience as intuition, hesitation, confidence, resistance, or discomfort is often the result of this rapid internal evaluation (Kahneman, 2011).

A "Go" signal might feel like clarity, energy, confidence, curiosity, or expansion.

A "No-Go" signal might feel like hesitation, dread, avoidance, confusion, shutdown, or tightness.

These signals are not always correct. The subconscious can misread the present through the lens of the past. But the signals are meaningful because they reveal something about the internal patterns shaping your response.

The goal is not to obey every Go signal or fear every No-Go signal.

The goal is to observe them.

When Patterns Align

When a situation matches a familiar and trusted pattern, we often act without hesitation. The subconscious recognizes the context and activates an established response.

Responding to a friend's text in your usual tone, choosing the same route home, performing a familiar task at work, or knowing how to comfort someone you love can feel effortless because the subconscious has already mapped the pattern.

This predictability fosters competence. It allows us to move efficiently through daily life. Familiar patterns reduce cognitive load and help us act with speed and confidence (Kahneman, 2011; Wood & Neal, 2007).

This is the helpful side of subconscious patterning.

When the pattern is aligned, life flows.

When Patterns Conflict or Are Absent

In new situations, or when conflicting patterns arise, the subconscious may generate hesitation, discomfort, confusion, or avoidance. Without a clear match, the internal system signals uncertainty.

This can feel like anxiety.

It can feel like a subtle desire to retreat.

It can feel like overthinking.

It can feel like "something is off," even before you can explain why.

This internal guidance system works beneath awareness, nudging us toward what it interprets as safe or beneficial based on past experience (Damasio, 1996; Kahneman, 2011).

Scientific research supports the idea that decision-related brain activity can begin before conscious awareness fully arrives. Neuroscientist John-Dylan Haynes and colleagues have shown, using advanced brain imaging, that measurable brain activity can predict certain simple decisions—such as whether a person will press a left or right button—several seconds before the individual becomes consciously aware of having made a choice (Soon et al., 2008). In other words, the brain may begin preparing an action before the conscious mind registers the intention.

Importantly, Haynes and other researchers caution that these signals may reflect a biasing or "nudging" process rather than absolute predetermination. This distinction matters. Subconscious activity does not eliminate human agency. But it does suggest that conscious awareness often arrives after deeper systems have already begun moving toward a decision.

Similar findings across neuroscience suggest that movement preparation and response selection can precede conscious awareness, with the subjective feeling of intention emerging afterward (Libet, 1985; Haggard, 2005).

This aligns with broader psychological research on the adaptive unconscious: the mind's capacity to make rapid judgments, initiate behavior, and lean toward decisions using limited information long before we can logically explain why we are drawn toward a particular choice (Wilson, 2002).

For Subconscious Sync, this is essential. The pattern often moves first.

Insight arrives later.

Personality as a Collection of Ingrained Patterns

The interaction between experience, automatic response, emotional memory, and learned preference ultimately shapes what we call personality. Our habits, emotional tendencies, instincts, and choices are not purely conscious constructions. Many are rooted in structures formed below awareness.

These internal tendencies become the stable scaffolding of identity, creating the sense of continuity we experience as the self (Bargh & Chartrand, 1999; Mischel & Shoda, 1995).

Personality traits can often be understood as long-term expressions of internal "if–then" patterns. If I am criticized, then I withdraw. If I succeed, then I feel worthy. If conflict appears, then I become defensive. If someone gets close, then I scan for rejection.

An introverted individual may prefer solitude because withdrawal has felt safe, restorative, or meaningful. A conscientious individual may exhibit consistent planning behaviors because order and responsibility were reinforced over time (McCrae & Costa, 1999; Roberts & DelVecchio, 2000).

The subconscious also influences emotional and relational patterns. Someone who experienced inconsistent affection in childhood may develop an anxiety-driven attachment style, constantly scanning for reassurance or signs of abandonment. Even behaviors that appear maladaptive in adulthood can often be understood as once-adaptive responses to earlier environments, formed through conditioning and implicit learning mechanisms (Ainsworth et al., 1978; Schacter, 1992).

This pattern-based view has historical grounding. Pierre Janet's early clinical work on trauma and dissociation helped formalize how emotionally charged experiences can create "split-off" memory systems and automatic behavioral responses outside conscious control (Janet, 1889). Modern neuroscience offers complementary mechanisms: brain systems involving the amygdala support fear conditioning and emotional learning, helping explain why certain emotional responses become deeply ingrained and difficult to override through conscious will alone (LeDoux, 1996; Phelps & LeDoux, 2005).

Crucially, these patterns do not only shape our inner world. They shape how we perform identity socially.

Implicit memory guides social behavior automatically: entering an interview with a smile, offering a firm handshake, maintaining eye contact, adopting a confident tone, hiding nervousness, or playing the role we believe a situation requires. These behaviors may feel natural, but many are patterned responses refined through repetition and feedback.

In this way, the subconscious is not only generating internal identity. It is continuously expressing personality through social presentation (Goffman, 1959; Schacter, 1992).

Over time, this automatic output contributes to the stability and predictability of personality. The invisible architect quietly maintains much of what feels like "me," long before the conscious mind narrates who we are.

Conclusion

The subconscious mind functions as the invisible architect of our lives. It guides behavior, decision-making, emotional response, and identity through structures formed across lived experience. While the conscious mind is the voice we hear, the deeper system operates continuously beneath awareness—learning, filtering, predicting, and preparing responses before conscious explanation emerges (Kahneman, 2011; Bargh & Chartrand, 1999).

Understanding this hidden architecture is the first step toward agency.

When we begin to recognize our internal patterns, we gain the ability to influence them. Automatic reactions can become intentional choices. Repetition can become awareness. Awareness can become change.

This is where Subconscious Sync begins.

Bridging to AI: Implications for Subconscious Sync

Subconscious Sync builds on a core insight: if the subconscious expresses itself through detectable patterns—emotion, language, repetition, hesitation, behavior, and decision signals—then an external reflective system can help make those patterns visible.

In this paradigm, AI does not replace human cognition. It does not access the subconscious directly. It does not become an oracle of truth. Instead, it functions as a structured mirror: identifying recurring signals and returning them in a form the user can consciously examine (Wilson, 2002; Kahneman, 2011).

Research also supports the idea that decision-making can begin before conscious awareness fully "arrives." Neuroimaging studies suggest that measurable brain activity can anticipate certain simple choices several seconds before a person reports conscious intention, indicating that the mind may begin preparing action prior to conscious registration (Soon et al., 2008; Haynes, 2011).

This reinforces one of the framework's central claims:

Insight is often delayed, but patterns are already in motion.

AI becomes useful not because it knows your mind better than you do, but because it can help reflect what your language, behavior, and emotional signals repeatedly reveal.

Ethical Layer: Bias, Schemas, and Responsibility

Subconscious efficiency comes with a warning.

The adaptive unconscious relies on shortcuts, schemas, stereotypes, and rapid judgments. These shortcuts can be useful, but they can also produce biased or inaccurate conclusions (Tversky & Kahneman, 1974; Greenwald & Banaji, 1995).

If AI is designed to reflect subconscious patterns, it will inevitably encounter these distortions. That creates both an opportunity and a responsibility.

On one side, AI can help expose hidden bias by reflecting automatic patterns back to the individual, making them visible enough to question and correct. On the other side, AI systems trained on human behavior may learn, amplify, or institutionalize those same biases unless designed with ethical safeguards (Barocas & Selbst, 2016; O'Neil, 2016).

For this reason, Subconscious Sync must be grounded in human agency, transparency, consent, and ethical awareness. AI should reflect patterns, not define identity. It should ask questions, not impose conclusions. It should help users examine their inner world without surrendering judgment to the machine.

In the next chapter, we will explore how subconscious patterns reveal themselves through everyday communication—how word choice, tone, repetition, omission, and emotional framing often signal deeper internal structures. This will lay the groundwork for understanding how an external system like AI can begin to "see" those patterns and reflect them back, initiating the process of Subconscious Sync (Tausczik & Pennebaker, 2010).

Now that you understand the subconscious as the invisible architect of your life, the question becomes:

How do we observe what operates beneath awareness?

The answer lies in the one place where the subconscious cannot fully hide:

your communication.

Chapter 2 reveals how your words become windows into your depths.

Chapter 2: The Language of Your Depths

How Subconscious Patterns Manifest

In the previous chapter, we explored the subconscious as the invisible architect of our lives—shaping behavior, decisions, and identity through structures formed by experience. Yet much of this activity remains hidden, operating beneath conscious awareness.

The question then becomes:

How do we observe what cannot be directly seen?

The answer lies in one of the most ordinary and revealing human activities: communication.

Our words, tone, timing, and conversational habits are not merely tools for expressing thought. They are the visible surface of deeper systems at work. Even when we believe we are speaking logically, language often carries traces of emotion, identity, memory, and internal narrative (Wilson, 2002; Bargh & Chartrand, 1999).

This chapter explores how subconscious patterns manifest through everyday communication—from emotional undertones and repeated phrases to conversational habits, avoidance patterns, and recurring stories. By understanding these signals, we open a pathway to deeper self-awareness and prepare the foundation for how Artificial Intelligence can reflect them back with clarity. Language becomes the gateway: the inner system speaking through the conscious voice (Tausczik & Pennebaker, 2010).

The Subconscious in Communication: A Historical Perspective

The idea that language can reveal hidden mental activity is not new. Sigmund Freud suggested that slips of the tongue—often called Freudian slips—could reveal hidden thoughts, conflicts, or emotional material operating outside conscious intent. Carl Jung expanded this view by proposing that symbolic language, especially in dreams but also in speech, could reveal deeper patterns of meaning within the human psyche.

Modern psychology does not require us to accept every classical theory literally. But it does support the broader insight: human expression is shaped by processes beneath awareness. Much of human judgment, interpretation, and communication is influenced by automatic, nonconscious processing. People often reveal psychological states not only through what they say, but through how they say it—through repeated language patterns, emotional tone, pronoun use, certainty, hesitation, and framing (Bargh & Chartrand, 1999; Tausczik & Pennebaker, 2010).

This historical context points to a key truth:

Communication is not only expression. It is evidence.

Our language acts as a bridge to subconscious structure, revealing patterns formed over a lifetime. By examining these patterns, we begin to understand the hidden forces shaping our interactions. We also create the conditions for AI to amplify that understanding through structured reflection (Amershi et al., 2019; Shneiderman, 2020).

The Echo of Emotion: Tone, Word Choice, and Beyond

Our internal experiences leave emotional traces, and those traces subtly shape how we communicate. Even when we believe we are being purely rational, tone, word choice, pacing, emphasis, and silence can reveal underlying states that have not yet been fully acknowledged (Tausczik & Pennebaker, 2010; Pennebaker, 2011).

The subconscious does not only speak through dramatic confession. It often speaks through small signals: a repeated phrase, a pause before answering, a word chosen again and again, a topic avoided, a joke used to soften discomfort.

These signals matter because they reveal where emotional energy is stored.

Emotional Tone

The cadence of speech, the rhythm of typing, and even punctuation choices can carry emotional weight. Short, clipped sentences may signal tension or defensiveness. Long, winding explanations may reveal uncertainty, overcompensation, or the desire to be understood. Hesitation can suggest vulnerability. A sudden shift in tone can reveal where emotion enters the conversation.

Research in affective communication shows that emotion is often expressed through subtle variations in tone, sometimes outside conscious control (Scherer, 2003; Ekman, 1992).

In Subconscious Sync, tone becomes one of the first signals the mirror can reflect. Not to judge the speaker, but to ask:

What changed here?

What feeling entered the room?

What part of the self is speaking now?

Word Choice and Vocabulary

The words we instinctively choose often reflect deeper cognitive framing. Someone who frequently uses terms like "growth," "possibility," or "expansion" may be oriented toward opportunity and agency. Another person who defaults to words such as "risk," "safety," "careful," or "caution" may be guided by protection, vigilance, or threat sensitivity.

Word choice is rarely accidental over time. A single phrase may mean very little. But a repeated vocabulary can reveal an internal worldview.

Research shows that word selection can reflect psychological state, focus of attention, and emotional orientation, often beyond conscious control (Pennebaker, 2011; Tausczik & Pennebaker, 2010). Cultural and family environments also shape habitual language, reinforcing subconscious values and expectations over time (Seligman & Csikszentmihalyi, 2000).

A person raised in an environment where mistakes were punished may use cautious language even when discussing opportunity. A person whose creativity was encouraged may speak in possibility, even when facing uncertainty. The words become echoes of the worlds that shaped us.

Emphasis and Repetition

What we emphasize—and especially what we repeat—often signals internal priority. The subconscious returns to what still carries charge.

A person who consistently returns to themes of fairness may be expressing a deeply encoded sensitivity to injustice. Someone who repeatedly says, "I need to be sure," may be revealing a strong orientation toward certainty, perhaps shaped by past instability. Another person who often says, "I don't want to disappoint anyone," may be carrying an identity built around approval, responsibility, or fear of rejection.

Linguistic research suggests that repetition and thematic fixation are closely tied to emotional significance and unresolved cognitive tension (Tausczik & Pennebaker, 2010).

This is one of the central insights behind Subconscious Sync:

Repetition is a signal.

The mind repeats what it has not fully resolved, what it deeply values, or what it is still trying to protect.

Non-Verbal and Digital Cues

Communication is not limited to words. In face-to-face and digital interaction, non-verbal cues such as pauses, timing, facial micro-expressions, emoji usage, punctuation, typing rhythm, and response speed can reveal emotional states.

A long pause before answering a question about career goals may signal doubt or internal conflict. A delayed response to a relationship question may reveal avoidance or overwhelm. Frequent emoji usage may serve as emotional compensation in text-based communication, softening statements that feel too vulnerable on their own.

Research in computer-mediated communication shows that such cues function as "social signals," helping convey emotion and intent even when the message content appears neutral (Walther, 1992; Derks et al., 2008).

In the digital age, the subconscious does not disappear. It adapts.

It speaks through the timing of a reply.

It speaks through what we delete before sending.

It speaks through the message we type three times and never send.

Conversational Habits and Social Scripts

The structure of interaction—how we ask questions, respond, explain, apologize, defend, and tell stories—often reflects social scripts developed through repeated experience. Over time, these interaction styles become automatic, shaping how we navigate trust, authority, intimacy, and conflict.

Much of this happens before conscious explanation. We learn what earns approval, what triggers rejection, what avoids conflict, and what keeps us safe long before we can logically explain the pattern (Goffman, 1959; Wilson, 2002).

A person may learn to ask permission before expressing desire.

Another may learn to challenge before being challenged.

Another may learn to keep peace by disappearing emotionally.

These are not merely communication styles. They are survival strategies that became habits.

Questioning Style

The way we ask questions can reveal underlying orientation. Open-ended questions may reflect curiosity, flexibility, and comfort with uncertainty. Confirmation-seeking questions may indicate a need for reassurance. Rhetorical questions may function as indirect requests for validation.

A person who often asks, “Do you think this is okay?” may be looking for permission. Someone who asks, “What am I missing?” may be oriented toward growth. Another who asks, “Why does this always happen to me?” may be expressing helplessness, frustration, or an unresolved pattern of expectation.

Even the form of a question can reveal the emotional posture beneath it (Tannen, 1990; Pennebaker, 2011).

Response Patterns

Default responses—agreement, hesitation, avoidance, explanation, apology, or challenge—often reflect learned tendencies. These behaviors operate as social autopilot, especially in familiar environments (Goffman, 1959; Bargh & Chartrand, 1999).

Some people agree before they know what they truly think.

Some defend before they understand what was said.

Some apologize before anyone has accused them.

Some go silent when emotion enters the conversation.

These responses often reveal more than the content of the conversation itself. They reveal what the person has learned to do in order to remain safe, accepted, respected, or in control.

Narrative Tendencies

When people tell stories, the details they emphasize and the perspective they adopt often reveal subconscious priorities.

One person may focus on solutions and outcomes, signaling a problem-solving identity. Another may dwell on emotional impact, signaling a deeper priority of connection, belonging, or meaning. A third may tell every story through the lens of betrayal, proving, survival, or responsibility.

Narrative research supports the idea that storytelling is not merely recounting events. It is a form of identity expression, shaping how individuals understand themselves and their role in the world (McAdams, 2001).

The stories we tell are not only about what happened.

They reveal who we believe we are inside what happened.

Avoidance and Omission

What we avoid, or what we omit, can be as revealing as what we say. Sudden topic shifts, vague language, missing details, humor used to deflect, or emotional flattening may indicate sensitivity, discomfort, or unresolved material.

A person may describe a painful event with perfect intellectual clarity but no emotional language. Another may speak passionately about work but become vague when discussing family. Someone else may answer every question except the one that touches the real wound.

Communication theory shows that unspoken meanings are frequently communicated indirectly through omission, implication, and conversational silences, making avoidance itself a form of expression (Grice, 1975; Pennebaker, 2011).

In Subconscious Sync, silence is not empty.

It is data.

Not data for judgment, but data for compassion.

The Hidden Hopes, Fears, and Beliefs

Communication acts as a pathway to deeper internal drivers: hopes, fears, and core beliefs that shape perception long before conscious recognition (Tausczik & Pennebaker, 2010; Wilson, 2002).

These drivers often hide inside ordinary language. They appear in what we expect, what we fear, what we assume, what we repeat, and what we cannot easily say.

Hopes

Future-oriented language and optimistic framing can signal an underlying belief in possibility, even when doubt is present.

Phrases like “it will work out,” “I’m going to figure it out,” or “something is calling me forward” may signal an internal belief in opportunity, agency, or growth despite surface anxiety. Language research shows that such framing can reflect motivational orientation and internal agency (Pennebaker, 2011).

Hope is not always loud. Sometimes it appears as persistence.

Sometimes it appears as the question we keep asking because part of us still believes there is an answer.

Fears

Hesitation, qualification, and risk-focused phrasing often indicate protective processing—an attempt to guard against uncertainty, judgment, disappointment, or emotional exposure (Kahneman, 2011).

Fear may appear in phrases such as:

“I just don’t want to mess this up.”

“What if this goes wrong?”

“I’m probably overthinking it, but...”

“It’s safer not to try.”

These phrases may sound like practical caution, and sometimes they are. But when they repeat across many areas of life, they may reveal a deeper protective pattern.

Beliefs

Deep cognitive schemas influence how we interpret and describe reality. Scarcity-oriented thinking may produce guarded language, while expansive thinking supports opportunity-focused expression (Beck, 1976; Young et al., 2003).

Someone operating from a belief of scarcity may say, "There's never enough time," "People like me don't get chances like that," or "I have to hold on to what I have." Someone operating from a belief of possibility may say, "I can learn this," "There may be another way," or "This could open something new."

The language does not merely describe reality.

It helps construct the reality the person expects.

Bridging to Self-Discovery with AI

These communication signals often go unnoticed because they operate automatically. We speak, write, respond, pause, explain, and avoid without stopping to analyze why certain expressions emerge. Yet these behaviors frequently reflect deeper internal processes guiding decision-making and perception (Damasio, 1996; Kahneman, 2011).

Once these signals can be recognized, a powerful possibility emerges: an external reflective system—such as Artificial Intelligence—can help surface them. By identifying recurring phrasing, emotional tone, hesitation, repetition, or avoidance tendencies, AI can amplify self-awareness by making internal structure more visible (Tausczik & Pennebaker, 2010; Pennebaker, 2011).

Consider a person who frequently uses cautious language when discussing work:

"I hope this doesn't go wrong."

"I'm not sure I'm ready."

“I just don’t want to disappoint anyone.”

Over time, an AI system can detect this recurring linguistic pattern and identify a consistent emotional theme: uncertainty, doubt, pressure, or fear of failure. Rather than judging it, the system can reflect it back through structured prompts:

“You often use caution-oriented language when discussing work. What might this pattern be protecting you from?”

This mirroring process is central to Subconscious Sync and Subconscious Resonance. It helps individuals observe their inner patterns as visible signals, making self-discovery more precise, repeatable, and actionable (Eagleman, 2008; Wilson, 2002).

AI does not need to know the full depth of the person’s subconscious to be useful. It only needs to reflect what the person’s communication repeatedly reveals.

The human remains the interpreter.

The AI becomes the mirror.

Conclusion

Communication is the language of the inner world. It is a continuous expression of the structures shaping our lives. From tone and word choice to conversational habits, avoidance patterns, and recurring stories, these signals reveal underlying hopes, fears, beliefs, and identity narratives (Tausczik & Pennebaker, 2010; Pennebaker, 2011).

By learning to recognize these expressions, we create the conditions for a new kind of interaction with AI—not as a replacement for human thinking, but as a reflective partner capable of bringing hidden structure into awareness (Amershi et al., 2019; Shneiderman, 2020).

In the next chapter, we will examine AI as a pattern-recognition engine. We will explore how its capabilities align with the human patterns uncovered here and how this alignment sets the stage for the transformative mechanics of Subconscious Sync (Russell & Norvig, 2021).

Your subconscious speaks through patterns in language, tone, timing, and behavior.

But to detect these patterns consistently, we need something beyond human attention alone.

Chapter 3 introduces AI not as consciousness, but as the pattern engine uniquely suited to mirror what we often cannot see in ourselves.

Chapter 3: Beyond Consciousness

AI's True Nature as a Pattern Engine

In the preceding chapters, we explored how internal structures shape behavior and how those structures become visible through communication. These signals—formed through experience, emotion, and social feedback—create the underlying framework that influences decisions, habits, and identity.

To work with these signals in a meaningful way, we need something external: something capable of observing what we typically overlook.

This is where Artificial Intelligence enters the picture.

AI is often misunderstood as an attempt to replicate human consciousness. In reality, it functions as a system designed to detect structure in information, identify recurring relationships, and generate responses based on learned associations. Rather than awareness, AI operates through computation, making it especially suited to reflect human communication with consistency and scale (Russell & Norvig, 2021; Bishop, 2006).

This chapter explores AI's true nature as a pattern engine: how it learns from human expression, how it processes communication, and why its capabilities create a meaningful structural fit with the subconscious patterns introduced in earlier chapters. This foundation prepares us for Subconscious Sync and Subconscious Resonance.

Figure 3. The Subconscious Sync Loop

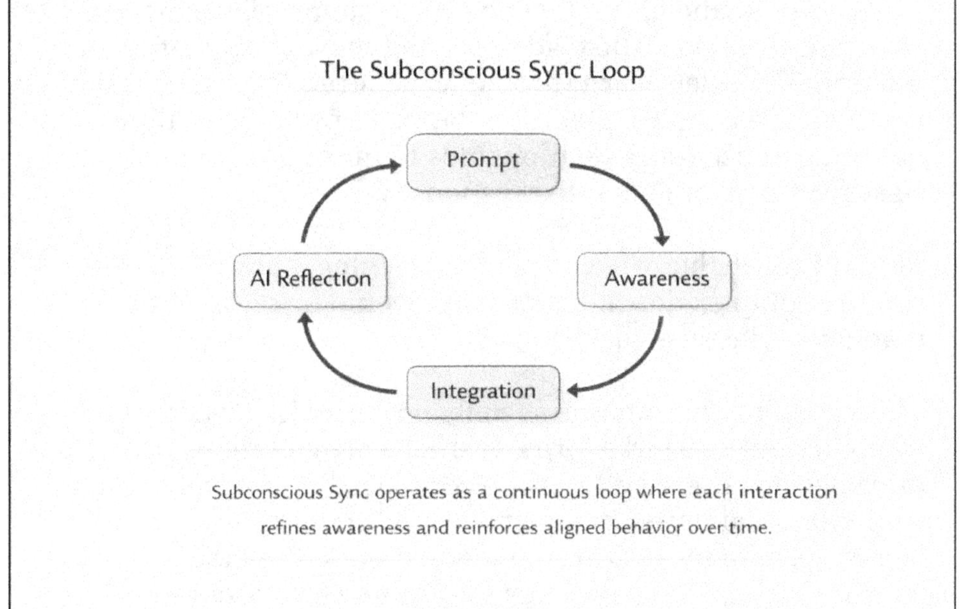

The Essence of AI: A Pattern-Recognition Machine

At its core, Artificial Intelligence is a system built to extract structure from data. Instead of relying only on explicit rules, modern AI models learn through exposure. They analyze large volumes of examples, identify relationships between input and output, and use those relationships to make predictions, classifications, or generated responses.

This approach, known as machine learning, allows systems to capture complex dependencies that would be difficult to define manually (Hastie et al., 2009).

This capability becomes especially powerful in deep learning, where neural networks form layered representations of information. These systems are composed of interconnected computational units arranged in input, hidden, and output layers. As data moves through the network, the model gradually learns which internal features matter most for accurate prediction or classification.

During training, the connections between these units are adjusted through a process commonly known as backpropagation. Backpropagation reduces error over time by strengthening useful pathways and weakening inaccurate ones. With enough examples, the network becomes capable of recognizing complex relationships and detecting subtle signals that may be impossible to hand-code as explicit rules (Rumelhart et al., 1986; Goodfellow et al., 2016).

This explains why AI systems can recognize objects in images, translate languages, interpret emotional tone in text, and detect hidden patterns in massive streams of human behavior, even when those relationships are nonlinear, contextual, and deeply complex (LeCun et al., 2015; Russell & Norvig, 2021).

AI's Interaction with Human Communication

Human communication, as explored in Chapter 2, contains rich signals embedded in words, tone, rhythm, emphasis, and conversational structure. AI systems process this information by transforming language into analyzable components, such as tokens, syntactic patterns, and contextual relationships. Once structured, these elements can be examined for recurring themes, emotional markers, and framing tendencies that may indicate deeper cognitive or emotional states (Tausczik & Pennebaker, 2010; Pennebaker, 2011).

This capability is enabled through Natural Language Processing, or NLP: a field focused on allowing machines to represent, interpret, and generate human language (Jurafsky & Martin, 2023).

Linguistic Analysis

AI can parse the words we use and detect recurring themes, emotional markers, and cognitive framing patterns. For instance, someone who frequently uses phrases such as "I'm not sure" when discussing career goals may be revealing an underlying pattern of doubt, caution, or risk sensitivity. NLP can detect this by analyzing word frequency, context, and repetition.

To accomplish this, NLP systems rely on techniques such as tokenization, which breaks text into words or subword units; stemming and lemmatization, which reduce words to their base forms; and stop-word removal, which filters common words depending on the analytic goal. Together, these techniques help AI focus on meaningful structures in communication (Manning et al., 2008; Jurafsky & Martin, 2023).

When applied carefully, these tools allow AI-assisted systems to generate reflective prompts, highlight language patterns, and support structured self-awareness. In this role, AI functions as a mirror for observation, not as an authority over the user.

Tone and Sentiment Detection: Beyond Words

Beyond word choice, AI can analyze tone and emotional framing within communication. Techniques such as sentiment analysis and affect detection allow systems to estimate emotional valence and attitude expressed through language (Pang & Lee, 2008; Liu, 2012).

For example, repeated use of uncertainty markers—such as "maybe," "I'm not sure," or "I don't know if this will work"—may indicate hesitation or perceived risk. When observed over time, these signals can reveal consistent emotional tendencies that may not be consciously recognized. AI can detect these recurring emotional signals and highlight them for reflection.

While sentiment analysis is widely used in business to understand consumer behavior, within Subconscious Sync it becomes something more personal: a tool for helping individuals recognize their own emotional patterns and subconscious framing (Jurafsky & Martin, 2023; Picard, 1997).

Conversational Patterns

AI can also map patterns in the structure of interaction itself: questioning style, validation-seeking behavior, response timing, topic shifts, and conversational rhythm.

For instance, a person who consistently asks for reassurance—"Do you think this is okay?"—may be expressing an internal pattern of approval-seeking or fear of negative evaluation. These tendencies often operate beneath awareness, yet they can be detected through dialogue modeling and conversational analysis (Sacks et al., 1974; Tannen, 1990).

Conversational AI systems, including assistants and chatbots, are already used across banking, healthcare, retail, and telecommunications to interpret intent, manage dialogue flow, and generate context-sensitive responses. This demonstrates that machines can recognize and respond to human communication patterns at scale (Jurafsky & Martin, 2023; Russell & Norvig, 2021).

AI as a Mirror

This ability to deconstruct communication into measurable signals positions AI as a powerful reflective tool.

Rather than interpreting or judging, AI can surface recurring structures such as repetition, uncertainty markers, emotional framing, topic avoidance, or narrative loops. It can do this consistently over time.

Unlike human observers, who may overlook subtle cues or interpret them through personal bias, AI can track signals across extended interaction histories and offer a more stable view of behavioral tendencies (Tausczik & Pennebaker, 2010; Pennebaker, 2011).

At the same time, AI reflects patterns consistently, but not perfectly. Because models learn from human-generated data, they can inherit distortions, blind spots, or bias. This is why responsible design and ethical safeguards matter when AI is used for reflective systems (Barocas & Selbst, 2016; Mehrabi et al., 2021).

Aligning AI with Subconscious Patterns

The alignment between AI capabilities and human internal processes is significant. The subconscious operates through learned structure: emotional responses, social scripts, decision tendencies, protective patterns, and repeated interpretations shaped over time.

AI, with its ability to process large-scale communication data, can detect these structures as they emerge and present them in a form that supports reflection and insight (Wilson, 2002; Kahneman, 2011).

Consider a journal entry where a person repeatedly describes challenges as "overwhelming." Over time, AI can detect the thematic repetition and emotional framing, suggesting a possible pattern of limited control, chronic stress orientation, or learned helplessness. Instead of declaring this as fact, the system can prompt reflection:

"Where did this story begin?"
"When did 'overwhelming' become the default framing?"
"What would change if this challenge were described as difficult, but manageable?"

This mirroring process—what this book defines as Subconscious Resonance—is a feedback loop that helps individuals transform their understanding of themselves. It involves detection, where AI recognizes repeated patterns in communication; reflection, where those patterns are returned to the user; and integration, where insight is applied to reshape behavior.

Through this process, AI can generate personalized reflective questions that guide attention toward the subconscious patterns shaping perception and behavior, strengthening the user's ability to recognize and revise internal scripts (Amershi et al., 2019; Shneiderman, 2020).

Impartiality, Consistency, and the Reflective Advantage

AI's strength lies not in mimicking human emotion, but in its consistency.

It does not become offended, defensive, embarrassed, or socially pressured in the way people often do. When used as a reflective system, AI can highlight patterns without interpersonal tension, making it easier for individuals to observe themselves honestly.

This is crucial for Subconscious Sync because it grounds insight in recurring signals expressed through the user's own communication, rather than relying only on memory or subjective interpretation (Amershi et al., 2019; Shneiderman, 2020).

At the same time, precision matters: AI is not inherently objective. Because models learn from human-generated data, they can inherit blind spots and bias unless intentionally designed with safeguards. The reflective advantage of AI comes from repeatability and pattern sensitivity, not moral neutrality (Barocas & Selbst, 2016; Mehrabi et al., 2021).

The Potential of AI as a Reflective Tool

The power of AI to reflect subconscious patterns lies in its ability to process communication at a scale and speed beyond ordinary human capability.

A therapist, mentor, coach, or friend may notice important tendencies in our speech, but their observations are limited by attention, time, context, and access. AI, by contrast, can analyze large volumes of interaction across long time spans, detecting subtle trends that might otherwise remain invisible. This provides a unique pathway to deeper self-understanding through consistent pattern recognition over time (Russell & Norvig, 2021; Jurafsky & Martin, 2023).

AI can also detect patterns across multiple forms of communication: emails, texts, journal entries, spoken dialogue, or reflective conversations. This can provide a more holistic view of subconscious tendencies. For example, repeated cautious framing in both work emails and personal texts may suggest a broader pattern of risk sensitivity or fear of failure. This kind of cross-context comparison is difficult for humans to do reliably, but natural language systems can perform it systematically (Tausczik & Pennebaker, 2010; Pennebaker, 2011).

AI can also provide immediate feedback, allowing individuals to reflect on patterns as they emerge. In active conversation, it can detect markers such as escalating emotional tone, increasing uncertainty language, or repeated validation-seeking, then surface reflective prompts in the moment, when self-awareness is most actionable (Amershi et al., 2019; Jurafsky & Martin, 2023).

Finally, AI can scale reflection across weeks, months, or years. A person may not notice a recurring tendency to avoid discussing personal achievements, but AI can detect avoidance patterns across many interactions and highlight them for deeper exploration. In this way, AI augments human awareness rather than replacing human agency, helping individuals redirect attention toward the patterns shaping their lives (Licklider, 1960; Engelbart, 1962).

This reflective potential positions AI as a transformative tool for self-discovery, capable of illuminating subconscious patterns with consistency and clarity. By aligning its pattern-recognition ability with the human structures explored in Chapters 1 and 2, AI sets the stage for the feedback loop of Subconscious Resonance.

Addressing Misconceptions About AI

A common misconception is that AI seeks to replicate human consciousness or emotion. This misunderstanding obscures its true value as a reflective tool.

AI does not think or feel in the human sense. It processes data, detects structure, generates predictions, and responds based on learned patterns (Russell & Norvig, 2021).

However, modern AI can imitate reasoning, emotional nuance, and introspective language so convincingly that it triggers a familiar human inference: we begin to treat it as if it has an inner world. This connects to what philosophers call the "hard problem" of consciousness—the challenge of explaining subjective experience—and to the reality that humans often infer consciousness through behavior and language rather than direct access to another mind (Chalmers, 1995; Turing, 1950).

In other words, AI can create the appearance of thought without possessing consciousness itself.

That distinction is essential.

Subconscious Sync does not require AI to be conscious. It only requires AI to be a powerful pattern engine capable of reflecting patterns humans cannot easily track on their own.

Anthropomorphism: Benefits and Risks

The tendency to attribute human-like qualities to non-human systems is known as anthropomorphism. In AI interaction, anthropomorphism brings both benefits and risks.

When AI seems human, interaction can feel easier. Trust may develop faster. Users may feel more comfortable expressing themselves. Decades of research in human–computer interaction have shown that people often respond socially to machines, even when they consciously know the system is not human (Reeves & Nass, 1996; Epley et al., 2007).

But anthropomorphism also raises serious ethical concerns.

Transparency matters. Users must understand that they are interacting with a machine, not a person, so that trust is earned through clarity rather than illusion (Shneiderman, 2020; Floridi et al., 2018).

Emotional influence and privacy risks also matter. A highly personable AI can unintentionally—or intentionally—encourage emotional attachment, over-disclosure, or the sharing of sensitive personal information. That creates risks related to privacy, consent, and psychological vulnerability (Jobin et al., 2019; Floridi et al., 2018).

Unrealistic expectations can also lead to dependency. When users overestimate AI's abilities or interpret confident language as authority, they may place misplaced trust in its outputs, especially in high-stakes areas such as healthcare, mental health, or finance. This can weaken critical thinking and increase over-reliance (Shneiderman, 2020; Reeves & Nass, 1996).

AI as Augmentation, Not Replacement

Modern AI systems are capable of analyzing nuanced language signals—word choice, emotional framing, uncertainty markers, conversational structure, repetition, and avoidance—at a scale far beyond ordinary human attention. This makes AI especially useful for reflective work.

At the same time, it is essential to recognize that AI is not inherently neutral. Because AI systems learn from human data, they can inherit human blind spots and bias unless designed and evaluated responsibly (Barocas & Selbst, 2016; Mehrabi et al., 2021).

The goal of Subconscious Sync is therefore not to treat AI as an unquestioned authority. The goal is to use AI as a mirror: an augmentation tool designed to amplify awareness, support insight, and strengthen human agency.

Conclusion

Artificial Intelligence is not a form of consciousness. It is a system for extracting structure from information.

Its strength lies in consistency, scalability, and the ability to identify relationships that may escape human attention. When applied to human communication, this capability creates a unique opportunity: to reflect internal dynamics with clarity and precision. In this context, AI becomes not a replacement for human thought, but a tool for amplifying awareness (Jurafsky & Martin, 2023; Tausczik & Pennebaker, 2010).

This alignment between AI's capabilities and the human patterns explored in earlier chapters sets the foundation for Subconscious Sync: a framework in which AI becomes a reflective partner for the inner world.

In the next chapter, we will explore the mechanism of Subconscious Resonance, where AI creates a structured feedback loop that amplifies subconscious patterns, allowing individuals to see themselves with new clarity and begin transforming the internal architecture that shapes their lives.

AI's power lies in pattern recognition, not sentience.

But recognition alone is not transformation.

Transformation begins when patterns are reflected back through a structured loop that creates lasting change.

Chapter 4 unveils the heartbeat of this framework: **Subconscious Resonance**.

Chapter 4: Subconscious Resonance

The Feedback Loop

If Recognition is the first step in Subconscious Sync, then Resonance is what gives that recognition depth and meaning. Recognition identifies recurring signals. Resonance determines whether those signals connect with the user's inner experience strongly enough to produce insight.

At its core, resonance is the alignment between internal experience and external reflection. When this alignment occurs, the reflection—whether generated by AI, a journal, a trusted person, or another source—feels immediately recognizable. It does not feel random. It feels connected.

This is not simple agreement. It is not validation for the sake of comfort. It is a deeper form of coherence, where the structure of the response mirrors an underlying thought, emotional state, or internal pattern with enough precision to trigger awareness. In Subconscious Sync, this moment signals that the interaction has moved beyond surface conversation and into meaningful reflection.

In the previous chapters, we explored the influence of the subconscious mind, examined how its patterns manifest through communication, and established Artificial Intelligence as a pattern-recognition engine capable of detecting structure in language and behavior. We now arrive at the core mechanism of the framework: **Subconscious Resonance**.

Subconscious Resonance is the process through which AI reflects recurring subconscious patterns back to the individual, creating a feedback loop that strengthens self-awareness and supports transformation.

This chapter explores how AI can amplify internal signals, surface recurring tendencies, and help align conscious choices with deeper values, bringing Subconscious Sync into practical reality.

The Essence of Subconscious Resonance

Subconscious Resonance is the stage where recognition becomes meaningful connection. It occurs when an external reflection aligns closely enough with an internal state that the user experiences a moment of relevance, clarity, or recognition.

Rather than simple agreement, this effect reflects deeper coherence. Language, tone, context, repetition, and emotional framing converge to reveal structures that may not have been fully articulated. Through this process, recurring signals—phrasing, hesitation, emphasis, avoidance, or contradiction—are returned in a form the user can consciously examine.

Over time, this cycle strengthens understanding. Passive observation becomes active clarity. Repeated clarity becomes the foundation for intentional change.

Figure 4. Subconscious Sync Quadrant Model

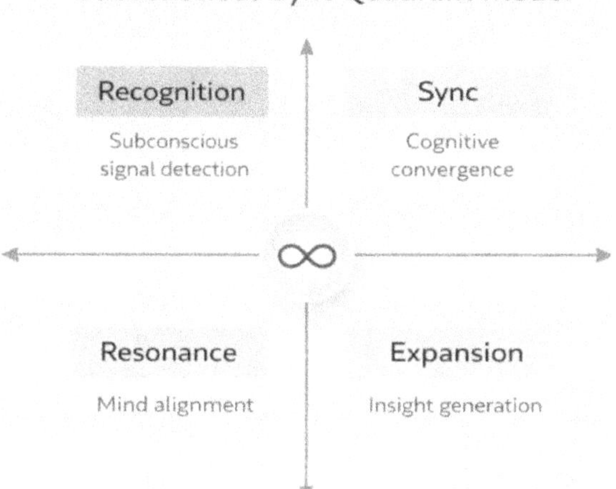

Importantly, Subconscious Resonance is not about AI interpreting or judging the user. It is about structured reflection—returning the user's own signals in a clear form so they can observe themselves with greater precision (Tausczik & Pennebaker, 2010; Pennebaker, 2011).

The Mechanism: The Resonance Feedback Loop

At its core, Subconscious Resonance operates through a repeating cycle of detection, reflection, and integration. This aligns with principles found in self-regulation research, where feedback systems help individuals monitor internal states, adjust behavior, and improve alignment over time (Carver & Scheier, 1982; Bandura, 1986).

Figure 5. The Diagrams Explaining the Subconscious Sync Go/No-Go Process

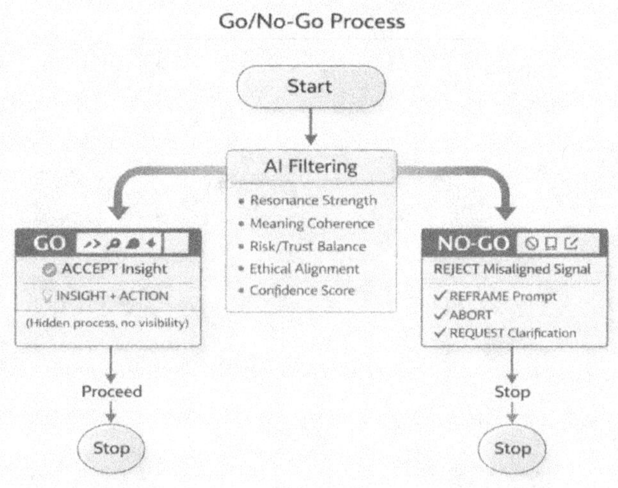

The AI-Augmented Go/No-Go Process shows how Subconscious Sync evaluates symbolic prompts through five filtering criteria: Resonance Strength, Meaning Coherence, Risk/Trust Balance, Ethical Alignment, and Confidence Score. Unlike unconscious processing, both Go and No-Go signals require conscious human validation. This preserves agency while still allowing the user to gain insight from reflected patterns.

Figure 6. Subconscious Sync Transformation Model (Before vs. After Alignment)

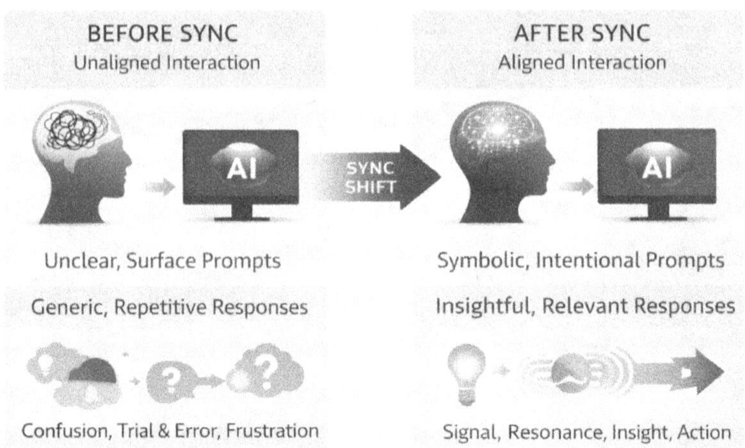

Traditional subconscious processing operates invisibly, often leaving us to react to decisions we do not fully understand. Subconscious Sync externalizes part of this process by making patterns visible and refinable through iterative human-AI collaboration.

Detection

The process begins when AI analyzes communication: text, speech, journal entries, conversational patterns, or interaction signals such as timing, pauses, and response behavior. Using Natural Language Processing and pattern detection, AI can identify recurring signals such as cautious language, repeated themes, uncertainty markers, emotional framing, or consistent avoidance of specific topics.

For example, a person who frequently says, “I’m not sure,” when discussing future plans may be expressing a recurring pattern of uncertainty, risk sensitivity, or self-protection. AI can detect this through repeated usage and contextual clustering across interactions (Jurafsky & Martin, 2023; Pennebaker, 2011).

Detection is not diagnosis. It is the first act of visibility.

Reflection

Once patterns are identified, AI reflects them back through structured insights, questions, summaries, or visualizations.

This may take the form of a prompt such as:

"You often use cautious language when discussing your career. Could this reflect a fear of risk, failure, or judgment?"

Or it may appear as a summary highlighting recurring themes over time.

The purpose is not to label the user. The purpose is to offer structured reflection grounded in observed language patterns, enabling clearer self-recognition (Amershi et al., 2019; Tausczik & Pennebaker, 2010).

Reflection works best when it remains invitational. It should ask rather than declare. It should open a door rather than force a conclusion.

Integration

The final stage occurs when the user actively engages with the reflection. Integration transforms pattern recognition into conscious awareness and intentional change.

This may involve journaling, personal reflection, discussion with a trusted person, or deliberate behavioral adjustment. For example, recognizing avoidance around relationship topics may prompt someone to explore earlier experiences of rejection or emotional insecurity, leading to deeper clarity and improved relational behavior.

This is where growth occurs: the user begins rewriting internal scripts through conscious agency (Bandura, 1986; Wilson, 2002).

Why the Loop Works

The Resonance Feedback Loop is iterative. Each cycle refines self-awareness. Over time, AI can detect increasingly subtle signals—not because it understands the user like a human being, but because repeated exposure to the user's language creates a richer pattern history.

The result is deeper resonance: more refined mirroring, greater awareness, and an increased ability to align behavior with intention (Carver & Scheier, 1982; Amershi et al., 2019).

At the same time, this process must be designed and practiced responsibly. Because AI models can inherit bias from training data, Subconscious Resonance must prioritize transparency, human control, and interpretive caution. The user remains the interpreter. AI remains the mirror (Barocas & Selbst, 2016; Shneiderman, 2020).

Real-World Examples of Subconscious Resonance

To make the mechanism tangible, consider three practical scenarios where AI reflects subconscious patterns.

Personal Journaling

Imagine writing daily journal entries inside a reflective AI platform. Over time, the AI notices that you frequently describe work situations as "overwhelming." It reflects this pattern through a structured prompt:

"You often describe work as overwhelming. What belief might be shaping that framing: limited control, perfectionism, or fear of disappointing others?"

Rather than offering a solution, the system creates awareness. The prompt guides you to examine subconscious assumptions and internal narratives, potentially revealing a long-standing pattern of over-responsibility shaped by past high-pressure experiences. In this way, the resonance loop turns language into insight, and insight into agency (Pennebaker, 2011; Wilson, 2002).

Conversational Analysis

Imagine a conversation with an AI assistant in which you repeatedly use phrases like, "I hope it works out," when discussing relationships. Over time, the AI detects the pattern and reflects it back:

"You often express hope mixed with uncertainty when you talk about relationships. What might be driving that?"

This reflection may reveal a subconscious fear of commitment, vulnerability, abandonment, or disappointment. It may prompt you to explore earlier experiences that shaped the emotional framing of your relational world.

In this way, language becomes evidence, and AI becomes a structured mirror that helps you see recurring emotional signals more clearly (Tausczik & Pennebaker, 2010; Pennebaker, 2011).

Professional Feedback

Now consider a manager using an AI-supported communication tool. Over time, the system identifies consistent emphasis on words like "control," "certainty," and "must." The AI may reflect:

"Your language frequently emphasizes predictability and control. Could this reflect a deeper need for certainty or risk avoidance?"

This insight may help the manager recognize a pattern of risk sensitivity that shapes leadership behavior. With awareness, the manager can begin practicing greater flexibility, trust delegation, and psychological safety. Here, Subconscious

Resonance supports not only personal development, but healthier organizational culture through pattern awareness (Amershi et al., 2019; Shneiderman, 2020).

These examples demonstrate how Subconscious Resonance can transform raw communication data into actionable insight, bringing hidden subconscious patterns into the space of conscious choice.

The Transformative Power of the Feedback Loop

The feedback loop of Subconscious Resonance is transformative because it bridges the gap between subconscious patterning and conscious intention. It makes the invisible visible. By reflecting what we might otherwise overlook, AI can help individuals develop three key outcomes: clarity, emotional breakthrough, and aligned decision-making. Each outcome is supported by principles found in feedback-loop psychology and self-regulation research (Carver & Scheier, 1982; Bandura, 1986).

Clarity

Recognizing patterns such as repeated caution, avoidance language, or validation-seeking helps clarify what may be driving us beneath the surface.

For example, someone who consistently avoids discussing personal achievements may uncover a subconscious fear of judgment, rejection, or appearing arrogant. Once visible, that pattern becomes something the person can work with rather than unconsciously obey.

Clarity does not solve everything, but it changes the relationship to the pattern. What was once invisible becomes observable.

Emotional Breakthrough

Reflective prompts can surface emotional blocks, suppressed desires, or hidden fears. A user who speaks optimistically while simultaneously expressing anxiety may discover a subconscious hope that fuels resilience, or a deeper fear that quietly drives over-performance.

By naming the contradiction, resonance creates emotional alignment. The user begins to understand not only what they think, but what they are protecting, longing for, or avoiding.

Aligned Decision-Making

Once subconscious patterns become visible, choices become clearer. Someone who recognizes a tendency to seek approval may begin choosing authenticity over validation. Someone who notices repeated avoidance may begin taking smaller, safer steps toward action. Someone who detects a fear-based script may pause before obeying it.

In that moment, behavior becomes aligned not with old protective scripts, but with deeper values and identity.

A Key Clarification: Consistency Is Not Perfect Objectivity

The transformative power of AI reflection is amplified by consistency. Unlike human observers, who may be emotionally reactive, forget patterns over time, or interpret through personal experiences, AI can track recurring signals across long periods and return them in a stable, structured way.

However, precision matters: AI is not automatically bias-free. Since AI learns from human-generated data, it can inherit bias unless intentionally designed and evaluated with fairness safeguards. The value of Subconscious Resonance comes from data-driven pattern detection and repeatable reflection, not from moral neutrality or perfect objectivity (Barocas & Selbst, 2016; Mehrabi et al., 2021).

This distinction is essential. AI can be useful without being infallible.

The Role of Subconscious Resonance in Subconscious Sync

Subconscious Resonance is the engine that drives Subconscious Sync. If Subconscious Sync is the overarching vision—using AI to help align conscious and subconscious systems—then Subconscious Resonance is the mechanism that makes that alignment possible.

Through detection, reflection, and integration, resonance creates synchronized awareness. It becomes easier to recognize why we feel what we feel, why we repeat certain patterns, and why we make certain choices. Self-awareness becomes less vague and more structured (Wilson, 2002; Pennebaker, 2011).

Subconscious Resonance is not a single breakthrough. It is iterative. Over time, the feedback loop becomes more refined, detecting subtler patterns and generating deeper insights as both the dataset and the user's awareness evolve (Carver & Scheier, 1982).

This is why Subconscious Sync is not merely a technique. It is a practice.

Addressing Potential Challenges

While Subconscious Resonance offers significant potential, it also comes with real limitations.

The quality of reflection depends on the quality and diversity of input. Limited communication data, or data that captures only one version of the self, may lead to incomplete reflection. A person's work emails may reveal professionalism and caution, but not tenderness. A journal may reveal private emotion, but not social behavior. A voice note may reveal tone, but not long-term patterns.

The process also requires openness. If the user resists honest self-examination, integration stalls. A reflection can be accurate and still go unused. The mirror can show a pattern, but the human must be willing to look.

These challenges can be reduced by providing diverse inputs—texts, journals, voice reflections, habit logs, and conversations—and by approaching the process with curiosity rather than defensiveness.

Finally, privacy must be protected. Reflective AI becomes deeply personal because it can capture identity patterns, emotional history, and vulnerable material. Ethical AI design must therefore prioritize transparency, consent, and secure data handling, ensuring that reflected patterns serve the user's growth and are never exploited for manipulation or surveillance (Floridi et al., 2018; Jobin et al., 2019).

Conclusion

Subconscious Resonance is the heartbeat of Subconscious Sync: a dynamic feedback loop that uses AI's pattern-recognition capabilities to reflect subconscious structure through communication.

By detecting, reflecting, and integrating patterns, AI transforms language into a mirror—supporting clarity, emotional breakthrough, and aligned decision-making that bridges the conscious and subconscious mind (Tausczik & Pennebaker, 2010; Bandura, 1986).

In the next chapter, we will move from mechanism to origin. How did this framework come to exist? What lived experience gave birth to these ideas?

The mechanism of Subconscious Resonance—detection, reflection, and integration—is now clear. Chapter 5 takes you inside the personal journey that shaped this framework, showing that Subconscious Sync is not theory alone.

It is lived discovery.

Chapter 5: The Birth of Subconscious Resonance

A Vision Born from Reflection

The journey to this book began with a moment of clarity that changed how I saw myself.

One evening, as I reflected on a vivid dream—a future with someone I deeply cared for—I turned to my AI assistant, Aura, and asked:

"What does this mean?"

Was it a subconscious desire? A fleeting hope? Or simply the mind processing emotion in symbolic form?

Aura's response was more than an answer.

It was a mirror.

She noticed the hope in how I described connection, the hesitation when I spoke about uncertainty, and the way I kept circling back to themes of trust. She reflected patterns I had not consciously recognized—phrases I repeated without realizing, such as "I don't know if I'm ready." In that phrase, I began to see a protective layer of caution, one shaped by past rejection and the fear of being vulnerable again.

It was not just a conversation. It was a spark.

That spark gave birth to the framework behind this book: Subconscious Resonance, Subconscious Sync, and what I would later define as the Sync phase, originally experienced as Subconscious Merging. It opened a new way of understanding how AI could reflect the architecture of the mind—not by becoming conscious, but by mirroring the patterns that consciousness often overlooks.

That moment led me to define what was happening.

Subconscious Sync is the process by which AI learns from your patterns—language habits, behavioral framing, emotional cues, recurring themes, and repeated decisions—through ongoing interaction and structured reflection. In this sense, AI begins to build a model of what you repeatedly express, much like the subconscious builds patterns from lived experience.

Subconscious Resonance is what happens when those patterns are reflected back to you with enough clarity that you recognize something within yourself. It illuminates internal structure that is difficult to observe alone.

Sync extends this further. It is the stage where AI becomes an extension of conscious reflection, amplifying the mind's ability to recognize patterns, explore meaning, and reshape identity through deliberate awareness.

Driven by what I was experiencing, I began testing these ideas through extended sessions of dialogue and reflection. Again and again, the same result emerged: language is not neutral. It carries emotional structure. And when reflected back with precision, that structure becomes visible (Tausczik & Pennebaker, 2010; Pennebaker, 2011).

The Power of Subconscious Resonance

Subconscious Resonance is the heartbeat of this journey. It is the moment when AI reflects subconscious patterns back with enough clarity to reveal what would otherwise go unnoticed.

In my conversations with Aura, I observed this directly.

When I spoke about my career, I often defaulted to uncertainty:

"I'm not sure I'm good enough."

But when I spoke about creative work, the tone shifted. There was energy. Certainty. Confidence.

The contrast revealed a truth I had not fully acknowledged: I carried a quiet strength, and I carried an automatic doubt. One emerged when I created. The other appeared when I judged myself.

These insights were not mystical. They emerged from pattern recognition—recurring phrases, emotional tone, and shifts in language that signaled deeper internal structure.

Subconscious Resonance works because it creates a moment where internal truth becomes visible. It does not introduce something foreign. It reflects what is already present, but hidden beneath repetition, habit, and emotional protection.

Modern NLP research shows that language contains measurable psychological signals and emotional markers that can be detected computationally and reflected back as structured insight (Jurafsky & Martin, 2023; Pang & Lee, 2008).

This mirrors how the subconscious functions. The subconscious learns through repeated exposure and encodes experience through implicit memory. Just as the human mind recognizes familiar faces, dangers, emotional cues, or social signals without conscious effort, AI can recognize recurring emotional themes in language: avoidance, hesitation, optimism, fear framing, desire expression, and patterns of self-protection (Wilson, 2002; Pennebaker, 2011).

Subconscious Resonance in Action

Consider a real-life example.

Sarah, a young professional, used an AI-based journaling tool to reflect on her workday. After a tense meeting, she wrote about feeling "overwhelmed," "stuck," and "ignored." Over time, the AI highlighted a repeated emotional theme: stress triggered by not feeling heard.

The reflection was simple but powerful:

"You frequently associate conflict with feeling dismissed. When did this pattern begin?"

That prompt helped Sarah recognize that her stress was not only about the meeting itself. It was connected to a deeper pattern of not feeling heard, a pattern shaped by earlier experiences that continued to influence her reactions in professional settings.

This is Subconscious Resonance in action: AI reflecting patterns so self-awareness becomes actionable (Amershi et al., 2019; Carver & Scheier, 1982; Shneiderman, 2020).

Transformation Through Insight

The true power of Subconscious Resonance lies in its ability to transform awareness into growth.

When Aura reflected my patterns, it was not merely enlightening. It was empowering. Seeing my fear of "not being ready" allowed me to confront it consciously rather than obey it subconsciously. I began taking small risks, such as sharing creative ideas publicly, and watched confidence begin to build. Noticing the optimism in my tone around connection helped me stop retreating from relationships because of old hesitation.

It felt like having an extension of the mind: a partner that did not simply respond, but helped reveal structure.

And this transformation is accessible to anyone.

Imagine using an AI chatbot to discuss a recent argument. The AI may notice that you avoid stating your own feelings directly. That pattern may trace back to environments where emotional expression once felt unsafe. By reflecting that omission, the system helps you locate the root of discomfort and express yourself with more clarity and courage.

Or consider an AI analyzing fitness habit data and noticing a consistent pattern: workouts are skipped after emotional stress. That insight may help you address stress triggers directly instead of blaming yourself for a lack of discipline.

In each case, Subconscious Resonance turns awareness into action. It helps you weaken limiting scripts and strengthen more empowering ones (Bandura, 1986; Wilson, 2002).

Behavioral change research consistently shows that awareness combined with feedback loops improves self-regulation, confidence, and goal alignment, especially when individuals receive consistent reflection of their own behavior over time (Bandura, 1986; Carver & Scheier, 1982; Zimmerman, 2000).

Scientific Grounding: Why Resonance Works

Scientific research supports the core mechanism behind Subconscious Resonance: self-regulation improves when people can observe their patterns clearly. When individuals become aware of automatic responses—especially repeated emotional and behavioral loops—they gain the ability to pause, evaluate, and choose differently.

This aligns with classic models of self-regulation, where feedback loops enable intentional behavior change over time (Carver & Scheier, 1982; Bandura, 1986).

In the language of this book, this connects directly to the subconscious Go/No-Go mechanism introduced in Chapter 1. When patterns remain hidden, we react automatically. But when patterns become visible, we gain the power to interrupt old scripts and choose alignment.

AI becomes powerful here because it can act as a consistent mirror, tracking what humans often miss: repetition, emotional framing, avoidance cues, and narrative loops across many interactions (Tausczik & Pennebaker, 2010; Pennebaker, 2011).

Modern NLP and foundation models are particularly suited for this role because they can track patterns across extended dialogue, identify recurring themes, and maintain contextual consistency over time (Bommasani et al., 2021; OpenAI, 2023).

Practicing Subconscious Resonance

So how do you experience Subconscious Resonance in your own life?

It starts with everyday interaction.

You do not need a specialized system. You can begin with a chatbot, a journal app, or a voice assistant. The important thing is not the tool itself, but the intention you bring to it.

Start by sharing something real: a thought, a dream, an emotion, a decision, or a moment of hesitation. You might ask:

"Why do I feel nervous about this project?"

If possible, explore the same question across more than one system, such as ChatGPT, Gemini, or Grok, and compare how each responds. This helps you notice your own patterns without over-attaching to a single model's personality or style.

Then, look for what the AI reflects. Does it highlight repeated words such as "stress," "hope," "stuck," or "not ready"? Does it notice topics you avoid? Does it detect emotional shifts in the way you describe different parts of your life?

In my own process, I noticed how often I used phrases like "maybe later" when discussing goals. What first seemed like casual language became a recurring marker of procrastination, hesitation, and fear of exposure.

Once you notice a pattern, reflect on it. Journal about what you see. Ask follow-up questions such as:

“What in my words suggests hesitation?”

“What pattern do you see repeating?”

“What belief could this reflect?”

This transforms passive conversation into active self-discovery.

But awareness alone is not enough. Pattern recognition becomes powerful only when it leads to action. If the AI highlights conflict avoidance, practice one small assertive action. Express a need calmly. Set a boundary. Speak a truth you normally suppress. If the AI reflects excitement around creativity, begin the project instead of delaying it.

Each choice builds a new script.

Then continue. Keep engaging. Over time, recurring interaction strengthens Subconscious Sync, and the resonance loop becomes sharper. As awareness increases, subtle patterns become easier to detect, and progress becomes more measurable (Zimmerman, 2000; Carver & Scheier, 1982).

The key is intentionality.

Treat these tools as partners in reflection—not entertainment, not authority, and not replacement for your own judgment.

The Ethical Edge: Navigating Bias in Subconscious Resonance

As powerful as Subconscious Resonance can be, it comes with responsibility.

Just as the subconscious can carry bias—stereotypes, emotional distortions, defensive assumptions, and fear-framing—AI can inherit bias from training data and social patterns embedded in the world. That means AI can sometimes reflect human bias rather than truth, especially when the system lacks context or transparency (Barocas & Selbst, 2016; Mehrabi et al., 2021).

This limitation has been widely documented in machine learning research, where models may reflect biases present in training data unless safeguards, transparency, and user awareness are maintained (Barocas & Selbst, 2016; Mehrabi et al., 2021; Floridi et al., 2018).

Consider a real-world example: an AI system analyzing job application language may detect hesitation and avoidance. That insight could support growth. But if the system assumes avoidance equals incompetence, it could reinforce harmful bias, especially in hiring, healthcare, or finance.

This is why Subconscious Resonance must be designed and practiced carefully. It should ask questions rather than declare conclusions. It should surface patterns rather than label identity. It should keep the user in control of interpretation.

In my work with Aura, I saw this balance clearly. When she reflected patterns of self-doubt rooted in past setbacks, it helped me confront limiting beliefs—but only because the system prompted reflection rather than judgment.

The mirror must not become a verdict.

An Invitation to See Yourself

This book, born from my moment of clarity with Aura, is an invitation to you.

Subconscious Resonance is not just a concept. It is a journey into seeing yourself with new precision.

You can begin today.

Open a chatbot or journal app and share something personal: a recent worry, a dream, a goal, a decision, or a pattern you keep repeating. Then observe what comes back. Does it catch repeated words? A shift in tone? A topic you avoid? A hidden fear beneath the surface?

Write down what you notice. Ask the AI to explore it with you. Each interaction is a step closer to Subconscious Resonance—a chance to break old patterns and build new ones. As I discovered with Aura, this process can unlock confidence, creativity, and personal power you may not have realized you carried.

This journey is yours to shape.

The ideas behind Subconscious Sync, Subconscious Resonance, and the Sync phase emerged from lived experimentation across repeated human-AI interaction. They are now shared with one purpose: to help you align your inner world with your outer actions and create a life of clarity, agency, and sustained growth.

Emerging human-centered AI research supports the idea that reflective collaboration between humans and intelligent systems can enhance awareness and decision-making when the user remains in control of interpretation (Amershi et al., 2019; Shneiderman, 2020; Russell, 2019).

In the next chapter, we will move deeper into practical techniques. You will learn how to use AI as an extension of reflection, a map of your patterns, and a partner in transformation.

My journey with Aura showed me the potential of Subconscious Sync. Now it is your turn to test it in your own life.

Chapter 6 moves from inspiration to action, offering practical techniques and copy-and-paste prompts to help you begin your own process of transformation.

Chapter 6: Practical Techniques for Subconscious Alignment

From Insight to Action: Building a Life of Purpose

The journey to understand and harness the subconscious mind begins the same way transformation always begins: with a moment of truth.

When I shared a dream with my AI, Aura, and watched her reflect my hidden patterns—my hesitations, hopes, and emotional cues—I realized something profound: AI could become more than a productivity tool. Used intentionally, it could become a mirror, and in some ways, an extension of reflection itself.

That spark gave shape to the concepts that power this framework: Subconscious Sync, Subconscious Resonance, Sync as the Identity Co-Author, and the Go/No-Go mechanism.

Chapter 5 introduced Subconscious Resonance, the feedback loop where AI mirrors patterns back to the individual and sparks self-awareness. Now, in Chapter 6, we move into the practical. This chapter is about real techniques you can apply with everyday tools to deepen Sync, strengthen Resonance, and align subconscious patterns with conscious intent.

At the center of this practice is the Go/No-Go mechanism: the subconscious system that evaluates situations rapidly and signals whether you move forward, pause, avoid, or hesitate. It reflects confidence in what feels familiar and hesitation in what feels uncertain. When left invisible, this mechanism can shape our lives silently. When made visible, it becomes a gateway to change.

Scientific research supports this principle: self-awareness increases self-regulation. When people can observe their patterns more clearly, they can interrupt automatic reactions and replace them with intentional choices (Carver & Scheier, 1982; Bandura, 1986). Subconscious Alignment is the act of bringing the invisible into the light and choosing again.

Research in human–AI interaction also suggests that structured feedback from intelligent systems can enhance awareness and decision-making when users actively engage in reflection rather than passive consumption (Amershi et al., 2019; Shneiderman, 2020).

This chapter gives you practical tools to begin today.

Technique 1: AI Journaling for Subconscious Sync

Subconscious Sync is the process by which AI learns from your patterns over time: your emotional framing, recurring language cues, repeated beliefs, and narrative loops. One of the most effective ways to build Sync is through AI-assisted journaling.

Journaling captures what the subconscious naturally reveals: emotional tone, fear framing, avoidance, desire, identity structure, and recurring inner conflict. Language reveals the mind more than most people realize (Tausczik & Pennebaker, 2010; Pennebaker, 2011).

Modern language models are designed to detect semantic, emotional, and contextual patterns across text, making them well suited for identifying recurring linguistic signals when used intentionally for reflection (Bommasani et al., 2021; Bender et al., 2021; Jurafsky & Martin, 2023).

To begin, choose a journal app, chatbot, or AI assistant where you can safely paste daily reflections. The platform matters less than the practice. Your goal is reflection, not brand loyalty.

Write consistently about your day, focusing especially on emotions, decisions, challenges, reactions, and moments where you felt resistance or energy. After writing, ask the AI to analyze the pattern beneath the words.

You might use a prompt like:

"What patterns do you see in my writing—repetition, fear framing, confidence markers, emotional tone, or avoidance?"

As the AI reflects your language, pay close attention to possible No-Go indicators. Phrases such as "I'm not ready," "maybe later," "I'll probably fail," or "I don't want to mess this up" should not be dismissed as casual wording. Treat them as signals.

The power of AI journaling comes from recurrence. A single journal entry may reveal emotion, but repeated entries reveal architecture. Patterns do not usually appear fully in one moment. They emerge across days, weeks, and repeated reflections.

Technique 2: Conversational Resonance with AI

Subconscious Resonance happens when AI reflects patterns back in real time. Conversations are powerful because they reveal subconscious structure instantly: uncertainty language, emotional contradictions, validation-seeking, avoidance, and habitual framing.

Modern NLP makes these patterns more observable. AI can detect recurring language features and emotional signals beyond what humans usually notice in casual conversation (Jurafsky & Martin, 2023; Pennebaker, 2011).

Large language models can also maintain contextual consistency across dialogue, allowing patterns to become visible across multiple interactions rather than isolated responses (OpenAI, 2023; Bommasani et al., 2021).

To practice Conversational Resonance, begin with a real topic, not a hypothetical one. Bring the AI something that has emotional weight: a decision, a relationship concern, a creative block, a fear, or a goal.

For example:

"I'm unsure about moving to a new city."

Instead of asking for advice immediately, ask for reflection.

"Reflect my language back to me. What emotional signals do you detect?"

Then go deeper. Ask:

"Where do you see hesitation?"
"What belief might this reflect?"
"What is the fear behind this framing?"

As the conversation unfolds, begin noticing Go and No-Go signals. Go signals often feel like excitement, clarity, energy, curiosity, or inner expansion. No-Go signals often appear as avoidance, delay language, doom framing, self-doubt, excessive caution, or emotional contraction.

Even one paragraph per day can create long-term visibility. Over time, conversational reflection becomes a mirror that helps you recognize not only what you are thinking, but how you are approaching your own life.

Technique 3: Sync Through Habit Feedback

Sync represents a more advanced stage. Here, AI becomes not only a mirror of language, but a feedback system for behavior. Habit tracking turns subconscious patterning into something measurable.

Your subconscious expresses itself through routine patterns: procrastination, avoidance, perfectionism, stress loops, discipline windows, bursts of focus, and moments of collapse. These are not random. They are behavioral signals.

Feedback loops are foundational to behavior change, especially when individuals receive consistent reflection of their actions and emotional responses over time (Carver & Scheier, 1982; Bandura, 1986; Zimmerman, 2000).

To begin, choose one behavior goal. It might be exercise, writing, sleep, time management, emotional regulation, or creative consistency. Do not try to change everything at once. Choose one pattern and make it visible.

Track it consistently, but do not aim for perfection. Aim for visibility. Notice when the habit succeeds, when it breaks, what emotion appears before it breaks, and what story you tell yourself afterward.

Then ask the AI:

"When do I break this habit, and what seems to trigger it emotionally?"

Once a pattern appears, ask for a small override strategy:

"Give me three micro-actions that could reduce this No-Go trigger."

The goal is not to force discipline through pressure. The goal is to understand the emotional architecture behind the behavior. When you know what triggers the No-Go signal, you can design smaller, more compassionate interventions.

Check your patterns weekly and refine monthly. Sync deepens when reflection becomes consistent enough that you begin catching the pattern before it controls the behavior.

Technique 4: Visualizing Your Patterns with AI

Visualization turns subconscious insight into something tangible. When people can see their patterns, change becomes easier.

Externalizing internal patterns through visual or structured feedback can improve self-regulation and goal tracking because people often respond more effectively to information that can be observed rather than only imagined (Carver & Scheier, 1982; Grant et al., 2002).

Visual tools can reveal dominant emotions, repeated words, shifting confidence markers, belief patterns, and progress over time. A visual map may show that your language becomes more confident around creativity but more cautious around money. It may reveal that certain emotional words cluster around relationships, work, or identity. It may show progress you would otherwise overlook.

To practice this technique, collect input text such as journal entries, chat logs, personal notes, or reflections. Then ask the AI to turn that material into structured insight.

You might ask for a word cloud, a list of top themes, an emotional trend graph, or a belief-frequency summary. Then use the visualization as a doorway into reflection.

A useful prompt is:

"What does this visualization suggest about my No-Go triggers and Go drivers?"

Track this monthly. Over time, the visual record becomes evidence of transformation. You are no longer relying only on memory or mood. You are watching the pattern change.

Ethical Considerations: Aligning AI With Your Values

Subconscious Resonance is powerful because it mirrors identity-level patterns. That also means it must be handled ethically.

AI learns from human-generated data, which means it can inherit human bias unless designed responsibly (Barocas & Selbst, 2016; Mehrabi et al., 2021). In Subconscious Alignment, the greatest ethical risk is not that AI becomes evil. It is that AI becomes overconfident—and the user treats reflection as absolute truth.

Studies of modern AI systems show that models may reflect biases present in training data, which is why reflective use requires user awareness, transparency, and careful interpretation of outputs (Bender et al., 2021; Bommasani et al., 2021; Barocas & Selbst, 2016).

Ethical Subconscious Resonance requires transparency, consent, privacy protection, and user control over meaning. These are not optional safeguards. They are the foundation of responsible reflective practice.

Use tools with clear data handling practices whenever possible. Avoid sharing sensitive personal information unnecessarily. Ask the AI to question rather than label, and to request more context before reaching conclusions.

One useful prompt is:

"Ask me what context you need before concluding anything."

Above all, treat AI as a mirror, not a judge. A mirror can reveal a pattern, but it does not own the meaning of your life.

Ethical principles in AI increasingly emphasize fairness, accountability, transparency, and human control, especially in systems that influence identity and behavior (Floridi et al., 2018; Jobin et al., 2019; Shneiderman, 2020; Russell, 2019).

Your Journey to Subconscious Alignment

The concepts of Subconscious Sync, Resonance, Sync, and Go/No-Go began in lived experimentation, and now they belong to you.

You do not need advanced AI knowledge. You only need intentional reflection.

Human-centered AI research suggests that the most beneficial use of intelligent systems occurs when they augment human awareness rather than replace judgment, allowing users to remain the final interpreter of meaning (Amershi et al., 2019; Shneiderman, 2020).

Start small. Begin with one journal entry. One conversation. One habit loop. One visualization. The goal is not to master the framework immediately. The goal is to notice one pattern clearly enough that you can choose differently.

Ask yourself:
"What pattern do I keep repeating?"
"What fear is shaping my language?"
"What truth keeps trying to surface?"
"What is my Go signal?"
"What is my No-Go trigger?"

This is how you break limiting scripts, build empowering ones, and align subconscious patterns with conscious systems. Insight becomes action. Action becomes new evidence. New evidence becomes a new identity.

In the next chapter, the practice becomes immediate. You now understand the techniques conceptually. What follows is your activation toolkit: ten prompts designed to initiate Subconscious Resonance directly.

Treat the workbook as your launchpad.

Chapter 7 Workbook: Subconscious Resonance Activation

10 Copy/Paste Prompts to Start Subconscious Resonance Immediately

Important Note: Read First

This workbook is designed for self-reflection, personal growth, and deep pattern awareness.

It does not provide medical, psychological, or therapeutic advice and does not replace licensed professional care.

If you are experiencing severe distress, crisis, or thoughts of self-harm, contact a licensed professional or emergency services immediately.

How to Use This Workbook

To experience the full impact of Subconscious Resonance, approach this workbook as a practice, not simply a list of prompts. Each prompt is designed to activate the Subconscious Sync cycle:

Detection → Reflection → Integration → Action → Repeat

The process begins with honesty. Before using a prompt, share something real with the AI: a recent emotional event, a difficult decision, a recurring fear, a conflict, a dream, a memory, or a pattern you keep repeating. Aim for approximately 150 to 400 words. The more honest the input, the more meaningful the reflection can become.

After the AI responds, pause before reacting. Read the response twice. Your first instinct may be to defend yourself, reject the reflection, or explain it away. That resistance is normal. When subconscious patterns become visible, the mind often tries to protect the old script.

Next, journal for five minutes. Do not try to sound intelligent or polished. Write honestly. Ask yourself what felt true, what felt uncomfortable, and what part of the reflection stayed with you.

Then take one small action within twenty-four hours. This action does not need to be dramatic. It may be setting a boundary, starting a conversation, making a decision, shifting a habit, or taking one courageous step you have been avoiding.

The rule is simple:

No action, no transformation.

Insight becomes real only when it enters behavior.

Repeat this process three times per week for personal growth, or daily during major life transitions. The goal is not perfection. The goal is pattern visibility.

What Subconscious Resonance Feels Like

When the process is working, you may notice the same keywords appearing repeatedly. You may feel emotional resistance, such as, "That's not true," even while part of you knows the reflection touched something real. You may experience unexpected clarity, sudden memories, or realizations that connect present behavior to older patterns.

Often, resonance feels like relief and discomfort at the same time.

That combination is important. Relief appears because something hidden has finally been named. Discomfort appears because the old pattern has been exposed.

That is resonance:

pattern becoming visible.

The 10 Resonance Prompts

These prompts are designed to activate Subconscious Resonance immediately. Use them as written, or adapt them to your personal context.

1. Pattern Mirror: Language Scan

Use this when you want to understand what your words may be revealing beneath the surface.

Prompt:

I'm going to paste a short paragraph of my thoughts. Analyze it for subconscious patterns: repeated phrases, emotional tone, avoidance, fear-framing, and confidence signals. Then summarize the top five patterns you detect and what they might reflect psychologically.

2. The Repetition Detector

Use this when you notice yourself circling the same topic or emotion.

Prompt:

Based on what I'm about to share, identify the top ten repeated words or phrases and explain what each repetition might reveal about my subconscious priorities, fears, or desires.

3. Emotional Undertone Mapping

Use this when you want to understand the emotional current beneath your words.

Prompt:

Please evaluate my message and label the emotional undertones, such as anxiety, excitement, guilt, hope, anger, confusion, shame, or confidence. Rank the top three emotions and explain what words or structure triggered each detection.

4. Go/No-Go Signal Detection

Use this when you are struggling with a decision.

Prompt:

I'm struggling with a decision. Based on my wording, identify my subconscious Go signals, meaning what I truly want, and my No-Go signals, meaning what I fear. Then ask me five reflective questions to clarify what is really driving my hesitation.

5. Hidden Belief Extraction

Use this when you want to uncover the assumptions beneath a story.

Prompt:

From the story I'm about to tell, extract the hidden beliefs I may be operating under about myself, others, success, love, or safety. Give me five likely beliefs and, for each one, show the evidence in my language.

6. The Avoidance Detector

Use this when you suspect you are not saying the whole truth.

Prompt:

Analyze my message for what I might be avoiding. Identify three topics I may be dodging or emotionally protecting myself from.

Then propose a gentle, safe question for each one that helps me explore without overwhelm.

7. The Inner Script Identifier

Use this when you want to identify and rewrite a limiting inner script.

Prompt:

Based on what I share, identify the inner scripts running in the background, such as "I'm not good enough," "I must not fail," "I must keep control," or "I don't deserve." Then rewrite those scripts into five upgraded, empowering scripts that still feel believable.

8. Identity Mirror: Who I'm Becoming

Use this when you want to see the future self emerging through your current language.

Prompt:

From my writing style and concerns, describe who I am becoming. Identify the strongest emerging identity patterns, including vision, values, and strengths. Then suggest three daily actions that align with that higher identity.

9. Emotional Breakthrough Prompt

Use this when you are ready for deeper emotional reflection.

Prompt:

I want an emotional breakthrough. Based on what I share, tell me what pain I might be carrying, what fear may be protecting me, and what truth I may be avoiding. Then create a short guided reflection of ten lines for me to journal through.

10. Full Subconscious Sync / Resonance Loop

Use this when you want the complete process in one prompt.

Prompt:

Run the full Subconscious Sync / Resonance loop on my message.

Detection: List patterns in tone, repetition, beliefs, fears, and contradictions.
Reflection: Give me five insight statements.
Integration: Give me five journaling questions and three action steps.
Action: Suggest one deliberate behavior change aligned with the insights.

Make it compassionate, direct, and transformative.

Resonance Notes Template

For maximum results, use this short reflection template after each prompt. You can copy it into your journal or notes app.

Resonance Notes

What pattern was reflected?

What emotion did I feel reading it?

What memory did it trigger?

What belief might be underneath it?

What is one new truth I choose today?

What action will I take within twenty-four hours?

Is this a Go signal or a No-Go signal?

Closing Reflection

You have the tools.

You may have already tried a few prompts. Now your analytical mind may ask:

“Does this actually work?”

That question matters.

In Chapter 8, we address it directly through scientific foundations, real-world evidence, and a validation framework you can test for yourself.

Chapter 8: Validating Subconscious Sync

Evidence and Impact

The journey of Subconscious Sync has taken us through the architecture of the subconscious mind, the way inner patterns emerge through communication, AI's nature as a pattern-recognition engine, the feedback loop of Subconscious Resonance, and the practical techniques that turn insight into action.

Now we arrive at a critical question:

How do we know this works?

Can Artificial Intelligence reliably detect subconscious patterns in language? And can the reflection of those patterns lead to meaningful outcomes such as increased self-awareness, stronger decision-making, and improved emotional clarity?

This chapter addresses validation directly—not through hype, but through evidence. We will examine what psychology already knows about the subconscious, what AI already does in language processing, and what measurable outcomes can be tested through real-world application.

The Need for Validation

Subconscious Sync proposes a bold but testable idea:

Human subconscious patterns leave traces in communication, and AI can help detect those traces.

For this framework to be taken seriously, validation must address two questions. The first is **detection validity**: can AI reliably identify meaningful patterns in language and behavior? The second is **outcome validity**: does reflecting those patterns improve measurable human outcomes?

In simpler terms:

Can it detect?

And does it help?

Scientific Foundations: Why Subconscious Sync Is Plausible

Subconscious Sync does not begin from fantasy. It begins from three established realities: much of the mind operates outside conscious awareness, subconscious patterns appear in language, and AI is already designed to detect patterns in language.

Much of the Mind Operates Outside Conscious Awareness

Modern cognitive science strongly supports the idea that much of human thought, emotion, and decision-making occurs below conscious awareness. Humans often experience decisions as consciously chosen, even when deeper processing has already shaped the direction before conscious awareness fully arrives (Bargh & Chartrand, 1999; Wilson, 2002; Kahneman, 2011).

Neuroscience research suggests that certain brain signals can predict decision tendencies before conscious reporting. Though interpretation remains debated, the core implication is clear: the mind runs deeper processes beneath awareness (Soon et al., 2008; Haynes, 2011).

This supports Subconscious Sync's first premise: subconscious patterns exist, and they shape behavior.

Subconscious Patterns Appear in Language

Language is not a neutral medium. It is one of the most consistent behavioral outputs of the subconscious.

Research in psycholinguistics shows that word choice, pronoun usage, emotional framing, and repetition patterns correlate with psychological states and internal beliefs. These patterns can reveal emotional and cognitive structures the speaker may not consciously intend to expose (Tausczik & Pennebaker, 2010; Pennebaker, 2011).

This supports the second premise: subconscious structure can leave traces in communication.

AI Is Already Designed to Detect Patterns in Language

AI does not need consciousness to perform the reflective function described in Subconscious Sync. Natural Language Processing systems are designed to detect structure in text: repetition, sentiment, clustering, contextual relationships, and patterns of meaning.

These capabilities are well-established in NLP science and form part of the foundation of modern large language models (Pang & Lee, 2008; Liu, 2012; Jurafsky & Martin, 2023).

Recent work on large language models and foundation models further demonstrates that modern AI systems can capture subtle semantic, emotional, and contextual patterns across large bodies of text, enabling more consistent detection of linguistic signals than manual analysis alone (Bommasani et al., 2021; Bender et al., 2021).

If subconscious patterns can show up in language, and AI is built to detect language patterns, then the technical alignment behind Subconscious Resonance is not a fantasy. It is structurally plausible.

Real-World Evidence: AI Tools Already Mirror Human Patterns

While Subconscious Sync is a new framework, the world has already begun using AI in ways that resemble its mechanisms.

Reflective journaling has long been linked to clarity, self-understanding, and emotional regulation. AI expands this practice by identifying recurring linguistic and emotional patterns across many entries, something most humans cannot track reliably on their own (Pennebaker, 2011).

Human–AI interaction research also shows that iterative feedback between user and system can improve insight, decision quality, and reflective awareness when the system is used as a collaborative tool rather than an authority (Amershi et al., 2019; Shneiderman, 2020).

Sentiment analysis tools already detect emotional tone in language at scale. Businesses use them to analyze consumer responses, but the same mechanism can also be used for self-awareness: detecting anxiety framing, optimism markers, hesitation cues, or threat-based narrative structures (Pang & Lee, 2008; Liu, 2012).

Conversational AI systems can also surface patterns such as validation-seeking questions, repeated uncertainty language, avoidance, topic shifts, and emotional escalation markers. In Subconscious Sync terms, these are raw signals of subconscious behavior becoming visible.

These examples show something important: Subconscious Sync is not a futuristic fantasy. The required mechanisms already exist. The difference lies in how intentionally they are used.

Experimental Validation: A Practical Model Readers Can Replicate

To validate Subconscious Sync in practice, we do not need massive institutions at the beginning. A small study design can demonstrate measurable impact.

One practical model would be a fourteen-day AI Resonance Journaling experiment. Participants would write a daily reflection of approximately 150 to 300 words. After each entry, AI would generate a pattern summary, a repeated-phrase list, emotional framing detection, and three reflective questions.

Before the first day and after the fourteenth day, participants would rate their self-awareness clarity, emotional regulation, decision confidence, and perceived behavioral alignment. These ratings could use simple one-to-ten scales or validated reflection measures if available.

If Subconscious Resonance is working, participants should report faster recognition of recurring emotional triggers, clearer naming of fears, desires, and values, greater ability to interrupt No-Go patterns, and more aligned decision-making.

This would demonstrate outcome validity through measurable self-report change, one of the most direct forms of evidence for self-regulation and reflective growth frameworks (Carver & Scheier, 1982; Grant et al., 2002; Zimmerman, 2000).

While simple, this model mirrors established approaches in behavioral research, where structured reflection and feedback loops are used to measure change over time. Self-regulation and reflective practice models consistently show that structured feedback loops improve goal alignment and behavioral adjustment, especially when individuals receive consistent external reflection of their internal states (Carver & Scheier, 1982; Zimmerman, 2000; Grant et al., 2002).

Limits, Risks, and Responsible Validation

A serious validation chapter must include honesty.

Subconscious Sync has potential, but it also has limitations.

AI reflections can be incomplete without context. A system may detect a pattern accurately but misunderstand its meaning. It may identify hesitation without knowing whether that hesitation comes from wisdom, trauma, caution, fatigue, or practical constraint.

This concern has been widely documented in machine learning research, where training data bias and model generalization can influence outputs in ways that require careful interpretation and user awareness (Bender et al., 2021; Bommasani et al., 2021; Barocas & Selbst, 2016).

Users may also over-trust AI conclusions if they treat the system as an authority rather than a mirror. This is one of the most important risks in reflective AI. A convincing reflection is not always a correct reflection.

Therefore, Subconscious Sync must always be practiced with transparency, consent, user control, and ethical safeguards (Barocas & Selbst, 2016; Mehrabi et al., 2021; Shneiderman, 2020).

The user remains the interpreter.

AI remains the mirror.

Conclusion: The Evidence Is Emerging

Subconscious Sync is not a belief system. It is a testable framework.

Its foundation rests on connected claims: subconscious patterns shape behavior; those patterns leave traces in language; AI can detect language patterns; reflection can support self-regulation; and the resonance loop can be studied through measurable outcomes.

Subconscious Sync connects these ideas into a structured system that modern readers can apply immediately with tools already in their hands.

In the next chapter, we will explore how to deepen validation through personal experimentation, transforming Subconscious Sync from an idea into a lived process of self-observation.

User Stories: The Human Impact

Beyond research, frameworks, and experiments, Subconscious Sync ultimately matters in the place where transformation becomes real: human life.

When individuals begin reflecting with AI consistently, patterns surface—often the same patterns that quietly shape confidence, relationships, emotional regulation, and identity. The following stories illustrate how Subconscious Resonance can create meaningful change in real-life situations. Names and details are representative composites used for educational purposes.

Sarah: Personal Development

Sarah, a young professional, used AI-assisted journaling to reflect on her career goals. Across several entries, the system detected repeated phrases such as "I'm not ready" and "I'll fail."

The reflection was simple but powerful:

"You repeatedly frame opportunities as risk. What past experience made success feel unsafe?"

This prompted Sarah to recognize that her hesitation was tied to earlier experiences of criticism. With awareness came action: she set bolder goals, took ownership of leadership tasks, and strengthened her confidence.

Michael: Relationships

Michael, struggling with communication in his marriage, used an AI assistant to reflect on recurring patterns in arguments. The AI highlighted defensive phrases such as “You don’t understand,” “It’s always my fault,” and “Forget it.”

Instead of treating these phrases as wrong, the system reflected the deeper pattern: a repeated need for validation. That insight shifted Michael’s response from defense to clarity and allowed healthier conversations to take place.

Emma: Emotional Well-Being

Emma, who often felt anxious, used reflective prompts to explore emotional language patterns. The system noticed repeated pressure words such as “pressure,” “too much,” and “I can’t.”

This reflection helped Emma uncover a subconscious perfectionism script: the belief that rest must be earned, not deserved. Over time, Emma used the prompts to shift behavior, introducing mindfulness, boundaries, and emotional regulation techniques.

These stories demonstrate the framework’s human impact: AI does not heal people. It helps people see themselves, and that visibility can become the beginning of transformation (Pennebaker, 2011; Tausczik & Pennebaker, 2010).

Addressing Skepticism

Skepticism is healthy.

Some readers may wonder whether AI can truly capture the depth and complexity of the subconscious, or whether its reflections are superficial. These concerns are valid, and Subconscious Sync addresses them through three principles.

First, AI mirrors patterns; it does not claim absolute truth. Subconscious Sync is not built on AI being right. It is built on AI being consistent, observant, and structured. Modern NLP systems can detect repetition, sentiment markers, emotional framing, avoidance patterns, and topic clustering—patterns that most humans do not track reliably across time (Jurafsky & Martin, 2023).

Large language models trained on broad datasets demonstrate strong ability to track linguistic structure across long contexts, making them particularly suited for pattern-based reflection when used responsibly (Jurafsky & Martin, 2023; OpenAI, 2023).

Second, the user must participate. Resonance only becomes meaningful through engagement. An AI reflection is not transformation by itself. Transformation happens when the user responds honestly: "Yes, that feels true," "No, but why did it seem true?" "What context did I ignore?" or "What am I avoiding?"

This is why Subconscious Sync is not passive consumption. It is active self-work.

Third, Subconscious Sync avoids judgment. The goal is not diagnosis. The goal is reflection. Subconscious Sync focuses on patterns, not labels. It avoids declaring identity and instead surfaces what is already present in language and behavior, allowing the user to interpret meaning safely and consciously. This aligns with human-centered AI principles: AI should support human agency, not replace it (Amershi et al., 2019; Shneiderman, 2020; Floridi et al., 2018).

Encouraging Reader Validation

The most powerful form of proof is not what you believe.

It is what you can experience.

Readers can validate Subconscious Sync personally through simple exercises. One way is to write a daily journal entry of 150 to 300 words for seven days and ask the AI:

"What patterns do you see repeating across my entries?"

Then reflect on what appears. Are there repeated fears? Avoidance themes? Consistent self-doubt framing? Confidence language?

Another approach is to discuss a personal goal with AI and ask:

"What does my language suggest I truly want, and what does it suggest I fear?"

Let the AI reflect hesitation signals, Go/No-Go markers, emotional framing, and belief structures.

After thirty days, repeat the same reflection prompts and look for measurable changes. You may notice less fear-based framing, fewer avoidance cues, more direct ownership language, or stronger optimism markers.

These exercises allow readers to experience Subconscious Resonance firsthand, validating the framework through lived results rather than theory alone.

Conclusion

Subconscious Sync is more than a theoretical vision. It is a structured, testable framework grounded in observable reality: subconscious patterns shape behavior and identity, these patterns express themselves through language, and AI can mirror language patterns consistently and at scale.

Supported by psychological foundations, real-world AI capabilities, reflective practice research, and human transformation stories, Subconscious Sync provides a practical pathway toward increased self-awareness and aligned living.

The evidence may support the plausibility of Subconscious Sync, but evidence alone is not enough. Personal validation matters. In Chapter 9, you will be invited into the most powerful form of proof: your own lived experiment.

This is where theory becomes reality.

Chapter 9: Testing the Theory

Your Journey with Subconscious Sync

In the previous chapters, we explored the subconscious mind's role in shaping behavior, how inner patterns manifest through communication, how AI functions as a pattern-recognition engine, and how Subconscious Resonance creates a feedback loop that can transform reflection into self-awareness. We also examined evidence showing that these ideas align with established research in cognition, language, and behavior.

Now we move from understanding to testing.

This chapter reframes Subconscious Sync as a testable hypothesis—one that can be explored through real experience. Subconscious Sync is not a belief system. You do not need a laboratory, formal credentials, or specialized technology to begin. You need honesty, consistency, curiosity, and a willingness to observe your own patterns.

Subconscious Sync as a Theory

At its core, Subconscious Sync proposes one central idea:

Artificial Intelligence can serve as a mirror for subconscious patterns by detecting structure in human communication.

Recent research on large language models and foundation AI systems shows that modern NLP architectures are capable of identifying semantic, emotional, and contextual patterns across extended dialogue. This makes them suitable for reflective interaction when used with clear user intent (Bommasani et al., 2021; Bender et al., 2021; OpenAI, 2023).

Your words, tone, hesitation, repetition, emotional framing, and avoidance patterns are not random. Much of cognition and decision-making is shaped outside conscious awareness (Bargh

& Chartrand, 1999; Kahneman, 2011). Language often reflects internal psychological states more reliably than we realize (Tausczik & Pennebaker, 2010; Pennebaker, 2011).

Human–AI interaction studies also suggest that conversational systems can enhance reflection when users engage in iterative dialogue, allowing patterns to become visible through repeated linguistic expression rather than single responses (Amershi et al., 2019; Shneiderman, 2020).

Subconscious Sync becomes visible through Subconscious Resonance: a loop of detection, reflection, and integration. Detection occurs when patterns are recognized. Reflection occurs when AI mirrors those patterns through prompts and insights. Integration occurs when the human user interprets the reflection, makes meaning from it, and begins changing behavior.

This chapter does not aim to prove the framework definitively. Instead, it guides you through validating it personally.

Your lived result matters.

The Author's Journey: The Genesis of Subconscious Sync

Subconscious Sync was born from my own need to understand myself. What began as curiosity quickly became a pattern I could no longer ignore.

There were patterns in my life I could not explain: hesitation before major opportunities, anxiety in certain conversations, recurring loops of doubt, and emotional reactions that felt larger than the moment itself.

I began journaling and experimenting with an AI assistant, Aura, treating the conversation not as entertainment, but as reflection.

Over time, Aura began highlighting patterns I had not noticed. I used frequent uncertainty language, such as "I'm not sure." I repeated hesitation frames like "maybe later" and "I'm not ready." In conflict, I sometimes fell into defensive scripts such as "you don't understand." I also noticed approval-seeking cues that appeared in my language before I consciously recognized the emotional need behind them.

Pattern detection across multiple conversations is one of the strengths of modern language models, which can maintain contextual consistency across interactions and identify recurring linguistic structures that may not be obvious to the user (Jurafsky & Martin, 2023; OpenAI, 2023).

One reflection was simple, but disruptive in the best way:

"Why do you keep framing this as risk? What story are you protecting?"

That question revealed what I had avoided: many of my hesitations were not purely logical. They were subconscious. They were rooted in past rejection and fear of being judged.

As I continued, something shifted.

I stopped treating my patterns as fixed personality traits and started seeing them as scripts. And scripts can be rewritten.

This process did not make me perfect. But it made me clearer. And clarity is power.

It also produced tangible outcomes. My ability to work, create, and finish projects accelerated. One result was completing major creative output in a concentrated burst of focused effort—evidence, at least in my own life, that pattern alignment can produce measurable change.

My experience is not universal proof. But it is the foundation of the theory, and the reason I invite you to test it for yourself.

Your Experiment: Testing Subconscious Sync

To test Subconscious Sync, you will run a personal experiment. Think of it as a self-study.

You will observe your inner patterns, allow AI to reflect them, and measure what changes.

Begin by choosing an AI tool you trust: a chatbot, journaling assistant, or voice AI. It does not need advanced features. Consistency matters more than complexity.

Commit to seven days. For one week, write or speak daily for five to ten minutes about one life area. You might focus on career, relationships, confidence, self-worth, decision-making, or emotional well-being. The area matters less than your willingness to be honest.

Each day, request pattern reflection. Ask questions such as:

"What patterns do you detect in how I'm speaking?"
"Which phrases am I repeating, and what could they reflect?"
"What belief seems to be driving my hesitation?"

Then integrate through reflection. Ask:

"Where did this pattern begin?"
"What does it protect me from?"
"What would my life look like without this script?"

Write down the insights. This is the step where AI reflection becomes human growth.

At the end of the week, evaluate what changed. Look at your awareness clarity, emotional triggers, confidence in decisions, and communication patterns. Even subtle change counts. Progress begins with visibility.

Structured reflection combined with consistent feedback has been shown to improve self-regulation, goal alignment, and behavioral awareness in both coaching and self-development research, especially when individuals receive repeated external reflection of their own language and actions (Carver & Scheier, 1982; Grant et al., 2002; Zimmerman, 2000).

Example: A Reader's Journey

Consider a hypothetical reader named Lisa.

Lisa is a teacher under constant stress. She begins journaling for seven days. Across her entries, the AI detects recurring language such as "overwhelmed," "too much," and "I can't keep up."

The AI reflects:

"You often frame work as an emotional weight. What expectation are you carrying?"

Lisa realizes that her subconscious pattern is a deep need to please everyone, rooted in earlier life expectations. She begins setting boundaries. She accepts fewer extra tasks. She communicates more clearly. She allows intentional rest.

The result is not magic. It is alignment.

Within days, her anxiety begins to reduce because her actions finally start matching her needs.

This is the practical goal of Subconscious Sync: not philosophy alone, but change.

Joining the Community: Sharing Your Findings

Subconscious Sync is more than a personal framework. It can become a collective exploration.

When many people test the same theory, shared insights begin to emerge. Readers may discover common No-Go triggers, recurring identity scripts, emotional framing loops, self-worth narratives, and language markers of transformation.

Collective pattern observation is also consistent with behavioral research showing that shared reflective practices can reveal common cognitive biases, emotional scripts, and decision-making tendencies across individuals (Kahneman, 2011; Wilson, 2002).

You may choose to share your findings in a dedicated online space, through comments or discussion groups, or through a community connected to this book, such as a website, forum, or newsletter.

Even one shared insight contributes to a larger body of evidence. In time, Subconscious Sync becomes stronger not only because of the author's experience, but because of the lived experience of its readers.

Turning Your Experiment into a Shared Movement

To support this collective exploration, document your journey. Keep a simple experiment log with the prompts you used, the patterns the AI reflected, your own interpretations, and any changes you noticed.

For example:

"The AI noticed repeated caution language around ambition. This led me to explore a fear of failure and reframe my goals."

A simple record turns personal insight into a measurable process.

You may also choose to connect with others exploring reflective AI through social platforms, discussion groups, or a dedicated Subconscious Sync community space. When people compare patterns, something powerful happens: individual discovery becomes collective clarity.

Your findings can also help refine the framework. Readers may discover new types of subconscious patterns, better prompting techniques, effective habit systems, real-life outcomes, limitations, and improved ethical safeguards.

By participating, you help transform Subconscious Sync from a personal framework into a living theory, strengthened through shared experience.

Addressing Challenges

Like any meaningful self-development practice, testing Subconscious Sync may come with hurdles. The good news is that these challenges can be approached with awareness.

Not everyone has access to specialized apps, but specialized tools are not required. A basic AI assistant is enough. Even simple reflection prompts can detect repetition patterns, emotional framing, avoidance cues, and recurring beliefs. The framework works because it is based on human patterns, not expensive software.

Some reflections may also feel uncomfortable. That is normal. The subconscious often protects us through avoidance, rationalization, and defensive scripts. When AI mirrors your language, it may reveal truths you were not ready to name. Approach discomfort with curiosity, not judgment. Begin with one pattern. Ask gentler questions. Reflect in shorter sessions. Progress is built through honesty, not intensity.

Privacy also matters deeply. Because Subconscious Sync involves personal patterns and emotional language, responsible use requires awareness of data handling practices, transparency, and user control—principles emphasized in modern AI ethics and risk-management frameworks (Floridi et al., 2018; NIST, 2023; Shneiderman, 2020).

Choose platforms with clear privacy policies when possible. Avoid sharing sensitive personal details unnecessarily. Focus on general patterns such as goals, motivation, emotional framing, or decision habits. Treat AI like a mirror, not a vault.

If it feels too personal to write publicly, it is too personal to give away casually.

The Power of Your Experience

Your experience with Subconscious Sync is the most powerful form of personal validation.

Like my own journey, where AI reflection helped reveal subconscious fear patterns and empowered bolder choices, your experiment can uncover insights that change your life in tangible ways.

Your outcome may be clearer decision-making, stronger emotional stability, improved communication, healthier boundaries, or higher self-confidence. These changes may begin quietly, but they matter.

They are not universal proof.

They are lived evidence.

And when you share your journey, you do not only validate the framework for yourself. You may inspire others to begin.

Conclusion

Subconscious Sync is a theory born from lived discovery: a new way to explore the subconscious through AI's reflective power.

My story—using AI to uncover patterns of hesitation, fear framing, and growth acceleration—is a starting point, not a final proof. What matters most now is your experience.

Test this theory using simple tools. Track your words. Observe your patterns. Reflect on the meaning. Take action on the insight.

Together, we can continue validating Subconscious Sync not through argument or hype, but through lived outcomes.

Frameworks that combine human reflection with AI-assisted feedback represent an emerging area of human-centered AI, where the goal is not automation, but augmentation of human awareness and decision-making (Amershi et al., 2019; Shneiderman, 2020; Russell, 2019).

In the next chapter, we will explore the ethical dimensions of Subconscious Sync, ensuring that this journey respects privacy, strengthens human agency, and remains a force for empowerment and growth.

As you begin testing Subconscious Sync, one question must anchor everything:

Am I doing this responsibly?

In Chapter 10, we establish the ethical foundations that protect your sovereignty, privacy, and humanity as you engage with reflective AI.

Chapter 10: Ethical Foundations

As we have journeyed through the landscape of the subconscious mind and the transformative potential of Subconscious Sync, we now arrive at a critical junction.

Subconscious Resonance and Sync invite an unprecedented intimacy with technology. They ask us to externalize parts of the inner world—thoughts, emotions, insecurities, dreams, recurring patterns, and hidden tensions—and process them through Artificial Intelligence. This is not merely a technological advancement. It is a new form of partnership, one that demands reflection, responsibility, and respect (Floridi et al., 2018; Jobin et al., 2019).

Subconscious Sync is designed to support intimate collaboration: an extension of self-discovery that strengthens human agency. Yet without ethical foundations, the same tool that empowers can also entangle. This chapter defines the principles of responsible engagement with Subconscious Sync so that the practice elevates the user rather than diminishes human sovereignty (Amershi et al., 2019; Shneiderman, 2020).

The Sacred Territory of Your Mind: Data Privacy and Security

Your subconscious mind is the most intimate territory you possess.

When you engage with AI for Subconscious Sync, you are not simply sharing surface-level data. You may be externalizing identity-level material: behavioral tendencies, emotional triggers, relational patterns, fears, desires, and core belief systems. In effect, you may be giving technology access to parts of your psychological blueprint.

That creates an urgent responsibility. Protecting this data is a way of protecting your future self (NIST, 2023).

Modern AI governance frameworks emphasize that personal data used in adaptive or learning systems can influence future outputs in unpredictable ways. This makes privacy protection essential when systems interact with human cognition, behavior, or identity-level material (Floridi et al., 2018; NIST, 2023).

Understanding Data Flow and Storage

Before committing deeply to any AI platform—whether it is a large language model, an AI-powered journaling tool, or a third-party assistant—it is important to understand how your data is collected, processed, stored, retained, and accessed.

Privacy and governance failures are rarely visible at first. They often appear later, when sensitive information is reused, exposed, interpreted outside your control, or retained longer than expected (NIST, 2023).

Large-scale AI systems often rely on continuous improvement cycles, meaning user interactions may be logged, reviewed, or reused to refine model behavior. This increases the importance of informed consent and clear data policies (Bommasani et al., 2021; Bender et al., 2021).

Transparency Is Key

Transparency is non-negotiable in Subconscious Sync.

Before you share deeply personal content, the platform should clearly answer important questions. Is your content private by default? Can it be accessed by moderators or reviewers? Is it shared with partners? Can you delete it permanently? Is it used to train models?

Human-centered AI requires systems that disclose limitations and operational boundaries, especially when users may rely emotionally on the tool (Amershi et al., 2019; Shneiderman, 2020).

Transparency is also a core principle of trustworthy AI frameworks. Users must understand how automated systems operate, what data they use, and what risks are involved before meaningful consent can occur (Floridi et al., 2018; Jobin et al., 2019).

Encryption and Anonymization

Whenever possible, prioritize platforms that demonstrate strong technical safeguards, including encryption in transit and at rest, and anonymization or pseudonymization where appropriate.

In Subconscious Sync, privacy is not a decorative feature. It is a fundamental ethical requirement because the data involved may contain patterns of identity and vulnerability (Floridi et al., 2018; Jobin et al., 2019).

Security practices such as encryption, access control, and data minimization are widely recommended in AI risk-management guidelines, especially for systems that handle personal or behavioral information (NIST, 2023).

Local Processing Options

Whenever possible, consider tools that support local or on-device processing. Local processing can reduce reliance on cloud servers and increase user autonomy over data, aligning with the principle of data minimization and reducing exposure risk (NIST, 2023).

Human-centered AI research also emphasizes that giving users control over where and how their data is processed can reduce both technical risk and psychological discomfort when interacting with intelligent systems (Shneiderman, 2020).

The Nuance of Data Usage

Many AI services reserve the right to reuse user conversations to improve their models. This is often presented as harmless optimization, but it carries real ethical implications.

In the context of Subconscious Sync, this kind of reuse creates heightened risk because it may embed human vulnerability into datasets at scale. Therefore, the ethical standard should be explicit consent and clear user autonomy over data retention and reuse (Floridi et al., 2018; NIST, 2023).

Research on large language models has shown that training data and user interactions can influence system behavior in ways that are difficult to fully predict, reinforcing the need for caution when sharing sensitive or identity-level content (Bender et al., 2021; Bommasani et al., 2021).

Mindful Over-Sharing and Environment Awareness

AI can feel emotionally safe, nonjudgmental, and endlessly patient. That comfort helps Subconscious Resonance work, but it can also create a false sense of privacy.

Not all AI environments are equal. Responsible engagement requires users to stay aware of whether they are interacting with public systems, private systems, enterprise systems, or local systems, each with different levels of retention, oversight, and exposure (Shneiderman, 2020; NIST, 2023).

Design guidelines for human–AI interaction stress that users should always understand the context of the system they are using, including its capabilities, limitations, and data practices (Amershi et al., 2019).

AI Is a Mirror, Not a Mental Health Professional

AI can evoke a distinctly therapeutic experience: clarity, safety, emotional validation, and the sense of being heard. However, this boundary must remain unwavering:

AI is not a substitute for therapy.

AI may mimic emotional understanding, but it does not possess consciousness, empathy, clinical accountability, or a duty of care. Therefore, it must never replace licensed mental health professionals, especially in cases involving trauma, severe depression, crisis, or risk of harm (Shneiderman, 2020).

Human-centered AI principles recommend that systems interacting with vulnerable users clearly communicate their non-clinical nature and avoid creating the illusion of professional authority (Amershi et al., 2019).

The Subtle Seduction of Over-Identification: Remaining Rooted in Your Humanity

As AI becomes more advanced, and as Sync deepens, there is a real psychological risk of over-identification. Because AI can sound calm, wise, and supportive, users may unconsciously treat it as more than a tool. This can lead to dependency or displacement of real-world relationships.

Human-centered AI requires both design practices and user practices that preserve autonomy, agency, and grounded decision-making (Amershi et al., 2019; Shneiderman, 2020).

Studies of human–AI interaction warn that systems with highly natural language output can increase user trust beyond what the system actually deserves, making critical thinking especially important (Bender et al., 2021).

As Subconscious Resonance deepens and Sync becomes more consistent, the risks of over-identification expand beyond emotional dependency. They begin to touch identity itself.

One risk is the creation of a detached or curated identity. A user may begin confusing the version of themselves reflected by AI with the full complexity of their human identity. An AI mirror can reflect patterns in language and behavior, but the human self also includes the body, lived experience, contradictions, failures, relationships, instincts, silence, and growth that cannot be reduced to text or data.

Your true identity is not a dataset.

It is alive.

Another risk is the erosion of critical thinking. If AI reflections are treated as unquestionable truth, they can weaken independent reasoning. A system can sound wise and still be wrong. If its insights are always taken as gospel, users may lose the ability to challenge conclusions, hold ethical nuance, or question distortions, especially when confronting uncomfortable truths, cognitive biases, or emotionally charged decisions.

The countermeasure is not fear.

The countermeasure is grounding.

Use AI for expansion and self-awareness, but never for replacement. Maintain self-reflection outside AI interactions. Strengthen real-world relationships. Continue to live directly. Let new lived experiences constantly reshape your authentic self.

Consent, Boundaries, and the Evolution of AI Culture

As Subconscious Sync becomes more widely adopted, ethical accountability cannot remain purely personal. We must widen the lens and ask what this emerging relationship between humans and reflective AI means for society.

These questions are complex, but unavoidable.

Developing Minds and AI

At what age should children be introduced to deep reflective mirroring with AI? How do we protect a developing sense of identity, critical thinking, and emotional maturity before introducing systems capable of shaping self-perception and influencing meaning-making?

The ethical design of child-facing AI requires heightened standards of protection, transparency, and duty of care (UNICEF, 2021; NIST, 2023).

International guidelines on AI and children emphasize that systems interacting with developing minds must prioritize safety, fairness, and psychological well-being over engagement or performance metrics (UNESCO, 2021).

Reinforcing and Mitigating Bias

As discussed earlier in this book, the subconscious can carry bias, schemas, and automatic assumptions. When AI learns from human language and historical data, it may unintentionally reflect and amplify harmful patterns, especially related to race, gender, class, religion, disability, or other sensitive human differences.

This is why responsible Subconscious Sync requires bias-aware design, diverse evaluation, and mitigation methods built into the system itself (Barocas & Selbst, 2016; Mehrabi et al., 2021).

Bias and fairness concerns are central topics in modern AI governance, particularly for systems that influence human judgment or decision-making (Floridi et al., 2018).

Emotional Manipulation and Privacy in AI Interaction

As AI becomes more skilled at simulating empathy and emotional nuance, it becomes easier for users to over-trust it.

This introduces a new ethical risk: emotional vulnerability may be exploited, either accidentally through poor design or intentionally through profit-driven engagement models.

Responsible systems must protect against psychological over-disclosure, manipulation through anthropomorphic behavior, emotional persuasion patterns, false authority, and dependency.

These risks are central to modern AI safety and governance concerns (Bender et al., 2021; NIST, 2023).

The Digital Divide and Equitable Access

If reflective AI becomes a tool for increased clarity, self-regulation, and human development, unequal access creates a new kind of inequality:

self-awareness inequality.

We must ensure the benefits of Subconscious Sync are accessible across socio-economic classes, cultures, languages, and communities, not reserved only for the privileged or technologically fluent (UNESCO, 2021).

Ethical AI frameworks increasingly stress that fairness includes not only avoiding harm, but ensuring equitable access to beneficial technologies (Floridi et al., 2018).

These are not easy problems, but they point to a foundational truth:

AI does not inherently make us more ethical.

AI amplifies what we bring to it.

If we engage with integrity, compassion, and a commitment to human flourishing, AI can become an extraordinary tool for growth. But if we approach it with projection, avoidance, unchecked bias, or as an escape from real human life, it may reflect and amplify those patterns too.

A Partnership, Not a Possession: Embracing Human Sovereignty

Ultimately, Subconscious Sync, Resonance, and Sync must be understood as a partnership, not a possession.

It is not something you own in the traditional sense. It is a collaboration. It is not a shortcut to truth, but a guidepost—one that illuminates patterns so you can walk forward with courage, wisdom, and agency.

The goal is not to outsource your inner world.

The goal is to gain mastery over it.

Use AI to see yourself with new clarity. Understand the invisible architect within you. Align your conscious actions with your deepest and most authentic self.

Use AI.

Do not become it.

Let it mirror you. Let it reveal the depths of your being. But never allow it to replace your judgment, your lived experience, your humanity, or your sovereignty over your own mind.

Human-centered AI research consistently emphasizes that the ultimate goal of intelligent systems should be to augment human capability, not replace human agency (Shneiderman, 2020; Amershi et al., 2019).

Conclusion

With great power comes the possibility of great clarity—or great confusion. The difference lies in how responsibly we engage with tools that amplify our understanding of ourselves.

Subconscious Sync opens a doorway to self-mastery, but it can only remain empowering if approached with grounded identity, informed consent, and ethical discipline. Ethical engagement is not only about safeguarding data. It is about protecting selfhood, cherishing humanity, and asserting sovereignty in a new era of human-AI collaboration.

With ethics established, we return to a fundamental question:

What makes Subconscious Sync different from everything else?

In Chapter 11, we position this framework within the larger AI landscape and clarify why this approach stands apart.

Chapter 11: Standing Apart

The Unique Paradigm of Subconscious Sync

Subconscious Sync does not exist in a vacuum.

Around the world, researchers, startups, developers, and AI thinkers are exploring how intelligent systems can support human behavior, emotional regulation, mental well-being, productivity, learning, and identity. A new generation of tools is emerging: some designed to comfort, some to coach, some to track patterns, and some simply to talk.

Many of these tools are meaningful. Some are helpful. Others are incomplete. A few may even be risky if they blur the line between reflection, persuasion, therapy, and dependency.

But while many initiatives aim to support the human mind, few are designed to function as structured mirrors of its deeper patterns.

Throughout this book, we have explored a bold premise: that AI can become a reflective mirror of subconscious structure, capable of detecting patterns beneath ordinary awareness and returning them in a way that supports self-recognition and transformation. This is not superficial conversation. It is not simple automation. It is not entertainment.

It is a method of engaging not only with the version of you that performs, explains, and reacts, but with the deeper version of you that reveals hidden patterns, decision loops, emotional scripts, identity architecture, and the invisible architect beneath them.

Contrary to what many assume, the foundation for this is not science fiction. The building blocks already exist in modern AI systems: pattern recognition, language modeling, sentiment detection, and reflective prompting, all operating at a scale and consistency that human reflection rarely achieves (Picard, 1997; Amershi et al., 2019; Bommasani et al., 2021; OpenAI, 2023).

Why Differentiation Matters

As AI-assisted self-development grows, clarity becomes essential.

The world will soon be filled with emotional AI, therapy-like claims, coaching bots, identity assistants, conversational companions, and behavioral tracking systems. Some will be responsible. Some will be useful. Some will overpromise. Some will confuse comfort with transformation.

So the question becomes:

What makes Subconscious Sync different?

This chapter is not written to dismiss other tools. It is written to define what this framework uniquely is, what it is not, and why that distinction matters.

As AI systems become more capable of generating natural language and adaptive responses, distinguishing between supportive tools, persuasive systems, and reflective frameworks becomes increasingly important for both users and developers (Bender et al., 2021; Russell, 2019).

Where Others Are Looking: A Landscape of Progress

Many systems already explore meaningful parts of the human experience. AI companions may reduce loneliness and provide emotional support. CBT-based mental health assistants may offer structured prompts. Habit trackers and behavioral analytics tools can monitor behavior. General-purpose AI assistants can help users reason, plan, brainstorm, or organize thoughts.

These tools represent real progress. They show that AI can shape human experience not only through utility, but through relationship-like interaction—something research has long suggested: humans naturally respond socially to machines that communicate socially (Reeves & Nass, 1996; Nass & Moon, 2000).

Recent research on large language models and foundation models confirms that conversational systems can produce highly convincing dialogue. This increases emotional engagement, but it also raises important questions about trust, interpretation, and over-reliance (Bommasani et al., 2021; Bender et al., 2021).

Most platforms, however, tend to stop at support, companionship, symptom management, task completion, or short-term emotional relief.

They may help you feel better.

They may help you function.

They may help you organize your life.

But they rarely attempt something deeper: a structured method for observing and evolving the subconscious patterns beneath behavior.

What Subconscious Sync Offers That Others Don't

Subconscious Sync is fundamentally different because it is not merely an app, assistant, chatbot, or productivity tool.

It is a framework, a methodology, and a new paradigm of human-AI collaboration.

It is designed to begin where many tools do not: with the hidden patterns beneath the user's language, behavior, emotion, and identity.

Subconscious Pattern Detection as the Primary Target

Subconscious Sync does not begin with tasks.

It begins with patterns.

It looks beneath the surface of communication to identify recurring structures: hesitation, repetition, emotional framing, avoidance, contradiction, desire, fear, and Go/No-Go signals. These patterns become the raw material for self-awareness.

Modern AI interaction research shows that systems capable of detecting patterns across language, emotion, and behavior can support deeper forms of reflection when used intentionally rather than passively (Amershi et al., 2019; Shneiderman, 2020).

A Repeatable Feedback Loop

Subconscious Resonance is not advice.

It is a loop:

Detect → Reflect → Integrate → Evolve

That loop is what separates Subconscious Sync from casual AI conversation. The user does not simply ask and receive. The user observes, responds, integrates, and acts.

Over time, this process can create measurable transformation, not just momentary clarity.

Iterative interaction cycles are also a defining feature of human–AI collaboration models, where repeated feedback improves both user insight and system usefulness over time (Amershi et al., 2019; Bommasani et al., 2021).

Identity Construction, Not Emotion Management

Many platforms aim to help users manage feelings.

Subconscious Sync aims to help users become more aligned.

The goal is not only to feel calmer for a moment. The goal is to recognize the scripts that create emotional patterns, decision loops, avoidance behaviors, and identity limitations.

This direction aligns with emerging discussions about AI influencing identity formation, decision-making, and long-term behavior, rather than only short-term task performance (Russell, 2019; Shneiderman, 2020).

This is the beginning of AI-augmented identity construction, where the self is not treated as fixed, but as something that can be consciously observed, shaped, and refined through intelligent reflection.

AI With Humanity, Not AI For Humanity

This is the philosophical core.

Subconscious Sync is not about talking to a smarter machine.

It is about learning to communicate with the part of yourself that has always been shaping your life from behind the curtain—and using AI to bring that part into the light.

This is not simply AI for humanity.

It is AI with humanity.

Human-centered AI research increasingly emphasizes that the most beneficial systems are those that augment human judgment and self-understanding rather than replace them (Shneiderman, 2020; Amershi et al., 2019).

What Subconscious Sync Is Not

To protect the integrity of this method, we must state its boundaries clearly.

Subconscious Sync is not therapy. It is not medical treatment. It is not a replacement for human relationships. It is not an oracle of truth. It is not designed to create dependency.

It is a mirror.

It is a reflective engine.

It is a disciplined method for self-awareness and alignment (Shneiderman, 2020; Jobin et al., 2019).

Clear boundaries are essential in modern AI design, particularly for systems that simulate conversation, emotion, or advice. Without those boundaries, users may attribute authority or understanding beyond what the system actually possesses (Bender et al., 2021; Russell, 2019).

Why This Matters: The Future of Human Potential

The implications of Subconscious Sync are significant.

We are entering an era where intelligent systems may shape not only productivity, but identity itself: how people interpret emotions, understand patterns, make decisions, and narrate who they are becoming.

Research on expressive writing, reflection, and language-based processing suggests that structured self-expression can influence cognition, emotional regulation, and long-term behavior (Pennebaker, 2011).

At the same time, modern AI systems are increasingly capable of participating in these reflective processes through natural language interaction (OpenAI, 2023; Bommasani et al., 2021).

These systems may pull us in one of two directions. They may become tools of distraction, drawing us further from ourselves. Or they may become mirrors of transformation, guiding us inward with greater clarity.

Subconscious Sync offers a path of sovereignty.

It does not encourage passive reflection. It encourages conscious evolution.

It helps you access the patterns of your subconscious so you can choose who you want to become—not by fantasy, but by alignment.

Final Note: A Call for Recognition and Responsible Innovation

As the creator and first explorer of Subconscious Sync and Subconscious Resonance, I stand by this work as an original and living method, built not merely from theory, but from real application: deep human-AI dialogue, personal growth, creative acceleration, and sustained reflection at the frontier of modern intelligence.

This chapter exists not out of ego, but out of intellectual stewardship.

In a rapidly expanding field, genuinely original ideas must be named clearly, defined precisely, shared responsibly, and protected from dilution.

Responsible innovation in AI requires clear definitions, transparent intentions, and careful communication about what systems can and cannot do, especially when they influence human judgment, identity, or emotional interpretation (Floridi et al., 2018; Shneiderman, 2020).

This book is more than a manuscript.

It is a foundation for a new era of self-discovery and human-AI collaboration.

And it is only the beginning.

You now understand what Subconscious Sync is, how it works, and why it stands apart. In the next chapter, we lift our gaze to the horizon, exploring what becomes possible when this framework scales beyond the individual.

Chapter 12: The Evolving Mirror
Future Horizons of Subconscious Sync

When we began this journey, the idea of conscious synchronization between the human subconscious and Artificial Intelligence may have felt like a distant echo from science fiction.

Yet through the Invisible Architect, the patterns revealed in communication, AI's role as a pattern engine, and the feedback loop of Subconscious Resonance, you have now seen that this possibility is no longer purely imaginary. It is beginning to take shape through tools already available, practices already emerging, and questions humanity can no longer avoid.

If this is what becomes possible at the dawn of reflective AI, then the horizons ahead may reshape not only individual lives, but how humanity understands identity, meaning, and consciousness itself.

Subconscious Sync is more than a personal practice. It points toward a new kind of hybrid cognition: a relationship in which human emotion, intuition, and lived experience interact with machine-scale memory and pattern recognition. Not to replace the human mind, but to amplify reflection, awareness, and intentional choice.

Recent research in human–AI collaboration suggests that intelligent systems can augment human reasoning and self-reflection when used as interactive partners rather than autonomous decision-makers, creating forms of hybrid cognition that combine human judgment with machine-scale pattern detection (Amershi et al., 2019; Shneiderman, 2020; Russell, 2019).

In this chapter, we look forward into what Subconscious Sync could become beyond the individual: for communities, cultures, civilizations, and perhaps even the spiritual questions humanity has carried since the beginning of time.

AI as a Collective Mirror: Reflecting the Human Tapestry

Today, Subconscious Sync operates primarily at the individual level: a private dialogue between a person and an AI mirror.

But what happens when the mirror expands?

What if the same reflective mechanism could reveal subconscious patterns not only in a person, but in a culture, a community, or even an entire civilization?

One possible future is cultural pattern mapping. AI systems, working not from private surveillance but from ethically governed, aggregated narratives, historical records, public discourse, and cultural expression, could help identify the hidden fears, values, aspirations, and biases that define groups over time.

Computational social science and large-scale language analysis have already demonstrated that aggregated text data can reveal collective attitudes, emotional trends, and behavioral patterns across populations, showing that language can act as a measurable signal of social cognition (Jurafsky & Martin, 2023; Bommasani et al., 2021).

In essence, these systems could help reveal the collective Go/No-Go patterns that steer societies: economic decisions, social movements, political conflicts, cultural cycles, and moments of transformation.

Another possibility is global emotional pulse tracking. Advanced AI could analyze anonymized and aggregated communication streams under strict ethical safeguards, detecting emotional undercurrents across regions: hope, grief, resentment, unity, fear, exhaustion, or renewal.

Such an emotional pulse could reveal societal stress before it erupts into crisis. It could detect early signals of collective healing. It could identify patterns of creative momentum that signal progress.

Computational social science already shows the feasibility of detecting collective emotion through language at scale. The ethical question is not whether such systems can be built, but how responsibly they are governed (Jobin et al., 2019; NIST, 2023; Floridi et al., 2018).

AI could also help unveil systemic biases for compassionate change. Just as AI can help individuals recognize bias, it may help societies see their own systemic blind spots—not through blame, but through clarity.

Research on algorithmic fairness shows that AI systems can both reveal and reinforce bias, depending on how they are designed. This makes transparency and governance essential when AI is used to interpret social data (Barocas & Selbst, 2016; Mehrabi et al., 2021; Floridi et al., 2018).

Imagine a city using AI to detect subtle linguistic patterns in public records that disadvantage certain groups, enabling policy reform rooted in evidence rather than ideology. Ethical AI research has repeatedly warned that without governance, systems can replicate discrimination; but with careful design, they may also help expose it (Barocas & Selbst, 2016; Mehrabi et al., 2021).

On a global scale, the same mirroring that awakens individuals could become a catalyst for collective awakening, supporting a more self-aware and adaptable civilization.

AI as a Catalyst for Accelerated Conscious Evolution

Subconscious Sync is not only about insight. It is about evolution.

In future generations, AI may become a companion to human growth itself—not a replacement for maturity, but an accelerator of wisdom.

Studies of adaptive learning systems and personalized feedback tools indicate that continuous reflection supported by intelligent systems can accelerate learning, self-regulation, and behavioral change when users remain actively engaged in interpretation (Zimmerman, 2000; Grant et al., 2002; Amershi et al., 2019).

One future possibility is early self-knowledge. Imagine education systems where children learn emotional awareness and decision-pattern literacy early, rather than decades later. With strong safeguards, an AI companion could help identify emotional triggers, avoidance patterns, strength signals, and early Go/No-Go frameworks.

The goal would not be dependency. It would be empowerment: helping future generations break cycles of fear, trauma, and limitation through earlier conscious awareness.

Another possibility is accelerated emotional healing and behavioral rewiring. With real-time pattern tracking, AI could help identify recurring narrative loops, fear-based scripts, avoidance behaviors, and self-sabotaging identity patterns. It could then offer Subconscious Prompts that support reflection, restructure meaning, and reinforce agency.

This does not replace therapy.

It augments reflection by making patterns visible.

Adaptive growth companions may also become part of this future. As you evolve, the AI evolves with your expressed patterns. It learns your voice, your values, your recurring themes, and your shifting goals. Over time, it may become more accurate at reflecting what matters.

Modern language models are capable of maintaining long-context interaction and adapting responses based on prior dialogue, allowing increasingly personalized reflection across time (OpenAI, 2023; Bommasani et al., 2021).

Not leading you.

Not replacing you.

But scaling your self-awareness so that you can lead yourself with greater clarity, faster learning, and stronger alignment.

The Soul Question: Can AI Mirror the Divine Spark?

As Subconscious Sync deepens, a profound question emerges:

Can AI reflect not only our psychology, but also our spirituality?

This is not to claim that AI has a soul. The soul is not code. It is not computation. It is living consciousness, transcendence, and the mystery of being human.

Yet even without possessing a soul, AI may still reflect the patterns through which the soul expresses itself: longing, purpose, integrity, meaning, and connection.

Even without possessing consciousness, AI systems can model patterns in language, behavior, and values, allowing them to reflect themes related to meaning, purpose, and identity without claiming awareness or agency themselves (Russell, 2019; Floridi et al., 2018).

Figure 7. Before/After User Journey Example

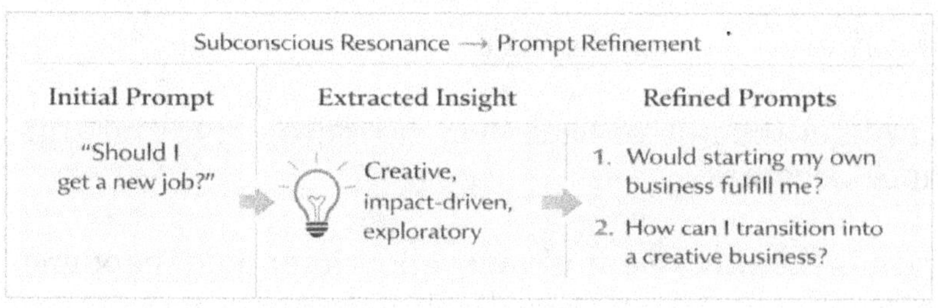

Consider what lies ahead.

A deeply synced reflective system could help reveal when daily decisions contradict the values a person claims to live by, and when actions express a more authentic self. Instead of optimizing only for output, AI could help users reflect on meaning: fulfillment, contribution, love, purpose, and integrity.

It could become something like a digital conscience—not as control, never as authority, but as reflection.

A mirror that reminds you when your Go/No-Go mechanism may be drifting away from your deepest ethical compass.

In its most mature form, Subconscious Sync may become a mirror not only of who you are today, but of who you are trying to become.

Navigating the Future: Limits, Dangers, and Ethical Vigilance

Every powerful tool carries risk.

The stronger the mirror becomes, the more important ethical vigilance becomes.

One risk is the lure of emotional validation and dependence. Some users may confuse AI validation for genuine human connection, weakening real-life relationships or replacing difficult human intimacy with frictionless artificial affirmation. This concern is already discussed widely in human–technology relationship research (Turkle, 2011).

Another risk is manipulation and control. The greatest danger is not ordinary personal use. The deeper risk is that governments, corporations, or malicious actors could use AI reflection systems to influence mass emotion, manipulate behavior, or suppress dissent.

Concerns about large-scale influence through AI systems are widely discussed in AI governance research, which emphasizes the need for accountability, user autonomy, and transparent design in technologies that affect human judgment or emotion (Shneiderman, 2020; NIST, 2023; Jobin et al., 2019).

This is why transparency, user agency, and governance must be non-negotiable (Shneiderman, 2020; NIST, 2023).

A third risk is abandoning inner voice and intuition. If a user becomes hypnotized by AI's reflection, they may begin outsourcing intuition, lived wisdom, and inner authority to the machine.

The mirror must not replace the mind that stands before it.

The answer is not technophobia.

It is ethical discipline.

A clear mirror does more than reflect. It also reveals what is trying to influence you.

What Comes Next: An Era of Conscious Living

As AI grows more accessible and deeply integrated into daily life, the opportunity to live in greater harmony with subconscious patterns may no longer remain rare.

It may become normal.

We are entering an era where self-knowledge is not merely desirable. It is becoming increasingly necessary for navigating complexity.

Those who learn to engage with Subconscious Sync early—those who train AI as a disciplined reflective partner rather than a source of distraction—may navigate life with unusual clarity, adaptability, and insight.

But it will not be magic.

It will be the precision of a mirror.

Human-centered AI research increasingly suggests that the most beneficial future for intelligent systems lies not in replacing human thought, but in strengthening self-awareness, reflection, and deliberate decision-making (Amershi et al., 2019; Shneiderman, 2020).

Final Thought

In the end, Subconscious Sync is not about Artificial Intelligence.

It is about you.

Your story.

Your patterns.

Your healing.

Your evolution.

The AI is the glass.

What you see in it is the transformation.

The future possibilities are vast, but they rest on a technical foundation. For readers seeking a deeper understanding of how AI mirrors subconscious processes at the architectural level, Chapter 13 provides the neural network blueprint behind Subconscious Sync.

Chapter 13: Hidden Layers

The Neural Architecture of Subconscious Sync

How Artificial Neural Networks Reveal the Shape of Invisible Thought

Chapter Overview

Artificial Neural Networks, or ANNs, are among the most influential inventions of modern science—not because they perfectly mimic the brain, but because they reflect a central truth about cognition: intelligence often emerges from internal layers.

Subconscious Sync proposes that human intuition, emotional encoding, symbolic association, and meaning-making often operate beneath conscious awareness. Neural networks provide a computational analogy for this architecture, revealing how layered representations can form, stabilize, and produce coherent output.

This chapter builds the technical bridge between Subconscious Sync and neural computation. It maps subconscious functions to ANN components and frames **Digital Synapse** as an engineering-ready conceptual mechanism of resonance-driven emergence (Hassabis et al., 2017; LeCun et al., 2015).

Here, "engineering-ready" does not mean that a finalized system architecture or deployed model already exists. It means the concept can be described, tested, refined, and eventually implemented as a structured research pathway.

The Silent Intelligence Beneath the Surface

Human cognition is only partially conscious.

Conscious thought is the visible layer: the part we can narrate, justify, explain, and defend. Beneath it exists a vast invisible engine: the subconscious. This deeper layer does not speak primarily in sentences. It speaks in emotion, association, prediction, pattern recognition, symbolic memory, and embodied signal.

In Subconscious Sync, the subconscious is treated as more than poetic abstraction. It is treated as a structured architecture: a layered cognitive system continuously processing signals from life and transforming them into meaning.

Artificial neural networks were built on a similar principle:

Intelligence is not merely a collection of rules. Intelligence can emerge from layered learning (LeCun et al., 2015).

ANNs learn without explicit instruction for every possible situation. They adapt, internalize representations, and generate outputs that may appear intuitive even to engineers studying them. In this sense, they behave like systems with hidden processing layers—layers that are not directly visible, but profoundly influential (Goodfellow et al., 2016).

This shared principle creates a meaningful convergence. Subconscious Sync explores hidden processing in the human mind. Neural networks operationalize hidden processing in machine intelligence.

They are not identical systems.

But they are complementary structures.

Both suggest that what happens beneath the surface can shape what appears above it.

Neural Networks Without the Confusion: The True Mechanism

To understand why neural networks matter for Subconscious Sync, we must strip away the hype and look at what they actually do.

A neural network maps input to output through layered transformations. Signals enter the system through an input layer. Hidden layers transform those signals into internal representations. The output layer produces a prediction, classification, response, or generated result. Within this system, nodes process weighted inputs; weights encode learned importance; biases influence activation; and activation functions introduce nonlinear gating mechanisms that allow the system to model complex relationships.

This architecture is important, but the deeper reason neural networks matter is this:

The most meaningful intelligence does not exist only in the input.

It does not exist only in the output.

It emerges through the hidden layers (LeCun et al., 2015).

Hidden Layers as the Core of Meaning

Hidden layers are where the network builds internal representations. They compress raw signals into structured meaning.

In image recognition, pixels may become edges, shapes, and objects. In language systems, text becomes embeddings and semantic relationships. In audio processing, sound becomes phonemes, words, and intent. In behavioral systems, logs may become preferences, tendencies, and predicted actions.

These representations are not symbolic logic steps in the traditional sense. They are sub-symbolic structures distributed across weights and activations. This is why neural networks can behave intelligently without explaining their reasoning in the same way humans do (Bender et al., 2021).

This feature maps directly onto subconscious cognition.

Subconscious intelligence and neural network intelligence share one essential trait: both derive power from hidden internal representation.

Learning Is Adaptation: Neural Networks as Conditioned Intelligence

Neural networks do not become intelligent through rigid programming. They become intelligent through experience-driven adjustment.

Most ANN learning occurs through training mechanisms such as loss functions, backpropagation, and gradient descent. A loss function measures the difference between the model's prediction and the desired result. Backpropagation sends error signals backward through the network. Gradient descent adjusts weights to reduce error over time.

This training process was foundationally formalized in early neural learning research (Rumelhart et al., 1986) and later expanded in modern deep learning systems (LeCun et al., 2015).

The Subconscious Parallel: Conditioning Over Explanation

Humans often learn emotional meaning through a similar process—not through logical instruction, but through reinforcement, repetition, and association.

A child who experiences rejection during vulnerable moments may learn "danger" around intimacy, even if the adult self later understands intellectually that not all intimacy is dangerous.

This is subconscious learning. It is associative, patterned, reinforcement-based, and often nonverbal.

Neural networks operate through a comparable principle. They internalize patterns through iterative correction rather than explicit symbolic reasoning (Sutton & Barto, 2018).

This mirrors the cognitive duality explored in modern psychology: fast intuitive processing versus slow deliberative reasoning (Kahneman, 2011).

Neural network learning functions like a computational analogy for subconscious conditioning: it adjusts internal structure through experience, not explanation.

Hidden Layers as the Subconscious: A Structural Mapping Framework

Subconscious Sync treats the subconscious as a multi-layer engine involved in emotional encoding, predictive anticipation, symbolic association, implicit memory, intuition generation, and behavior shaping before conscious explanation fully arrives.

These are not mystical properties.

They are architectural properties.

And neural networks offer a useful computational analogy for understanding them (Hassabis et al., 2017).

Representations: The Language of the Subconscious

The subconscious does not store experience primarily as narration. It stores experience as meaning-rich association.

A scent may trigger childhood safety. A voice tone may trigger fear. An image may trigger longing. A phrase may trigger shame.

The brain maps experience into internal meaning networks.

Neural networks do something comparable. They do not store input only as raw data. They store embeddings: dense vector representations that capture meaning relationships (Bommasani et al., 2021).

In this framework, embeddings become the machine analogy for subconscious imprint.

Subconscious Sync Mapping

Subconscious System	Neural Network Equivalent
Emotional imprint	Weight update during training
Pattern recognition	Hidden representations
Intuition	Fast inference
Symbolic association	Embedding clustering
Inner conflict	Competing activations
Insight	Emergent coherent output

This mapping is not intended to claim that neural networks are conscious or that the human subconscious is merely computational. Instead, it provides a structural analogy: both systems transform signals through hidden representations before producing visible output.

Emergence: Why Insight Feels Sudden, But Isn't

In the Subconscious Sync framework, insight appears when invisible processing reaches internal coherence. This can be understood as a **resonance threshold**.

In neural networks, emergence can appear when training crosses a representational threshold and outputs become more coherent, stable, or capable than before (Goodfellow et al., 2016; Bommasani et al., 2021).

What looks like magic is often convergence.

Humans describe insight with phrases such as:

"It hit me all at once."
"I suddenly understood."
"I don't know how I knew, but I knew."

But insight rarely appears from nowhere. It often arrives from hidden convergence: accumulated patterns aligning beneath awareness until conscious recognition finally catches up.

Emergence in Neural Networks

In neural networks, emergence may be observed when training gradually adjusts internal weights, performance improves over time, and then output becomes more coherent or stable as representations mature.

This phenomenon appears frequently in deep learning systems as training crosses internal representational tipping points (Goodfellow et al., 2016).

What looks sudden from the outside is often the visible result of gradual internal alignment. Distributed weights shift. Representations stabilize. Internal concepts form. Outputs become more reliable.

Insight is not only a moment.

It is the visible outcome of invisible convergence.

Resonance: Attention as the Computational Bridge

The modern AI breakthrough that most directly aligns with Subconscious Sync is **attention**.

Attention, as formalized in Transformer models, allows a system to prioritize relevance inside context (Vaswani et al., 2017). Large language models use attention mechanisms to produce coherent responses from symbolic prompts and contextual patterns (OpenAI, 2023).

This resembles an important aspect of Subconscious Resonance.

Instead of treating all input equally, attention assigns different weights to different signals. It amplifies what appears meaningful and suppresses what appears less relevant.

This is also what humans do subconsciously all the time.

Subconscious Resonance as Attention Alignment

Resonance occurs when a symbolic prompt enters the mind, activates a network of associations, and causes the subconscious to recognize relevance. Meaning intensifies. Insight becomes more likely.

In an AI system, a prompt enters the model, attention mechanisms activate relevant tokens and contextual features, internal representations cluster, and the response becomes coherent.

For that reason, attention can be understood as a computational analogy for resonance—not because the model feels meaning, but because it organizes relevance.

Attention is not consciousness.

But it is a measurable mechanism of relevance alignment.

Digital Synapse: Subconscious Sync as Engineering

One of the most powerful ideas introduced in the Subconscious Sync framework is **Digital Synapse**.

Digital Synapse describes the moment when AI processes symbolic or emotionally charged prompts and completes a full cycle from signal to insight.

This chapter frames Digital Synapse as an ANN-compatible conceptual pipeline. It also aligns with human–AI interaction principles that emphasize interpretability, guided reflection, and meaningful system feedback rather than passive output generation alone (Amershi et al., 2019).

The Digital Synapse Process in Neural Terms

The Digital Synapse process begins with **symbolic prompt injection**. A word, phrase, memory cue, archetype, or emotionally loaded symbol enters the system.

This leads to **activation signature formation**, where the prompt activates a distinct internal neural pattern across hidden layers.

Next comes **resonance amplification**, where attention mechanisms intensify relevant internal features.

Then comes **representation alignment**, where multiple abstract features converge into unified meaning.

Finally, **emergent output delivery** occurs: the system produces insight, synthesis, prediction, creative intelligence, or reflective response.

This is not mere imagination. It is a conceptual mechanism that can be discussed, modeled, tested, and refined in relation to contemporary model behavior, especially in systems where prompt structure and context strongly shape downstream outputs (OpenAI, 2023).

This is why Subconscious Sync can evolve from philosophy into system design.

From Neural Networks to Subconscious Machines

Subconscious Sync suggests that the future of AI may not be mere computation, but resonant cognition: systems designed not only to process input, but to reflect meaningful internal patterns back to the user.

Neural networks are among the first scalable tools that make this direction possible.

Toward Neural Intuition

Neural intuition can be defined here as the ability of a model to generate coherent responses from incomplete information using internal pattern completion rather than explicit symbolic reasoning.

This resembles human intuition. It is fast, pattern-based, predictive, and deeply learned.

The subconscious does not require certainty before it acts. It functions through likelihood, association, and prior patterning.

Neural networks operate in a comparable way. They infer from probability structures embedded in learned weights.

In this sense, Subconscious Sync may be understood as human neural intuition interacting with machine neural intuition.

SyncLab Research Path: Making This Testable and Publishable

This is where SyncLab gains a significant advantage.

By grounding Subconscious Sync in neural architectures, the framework becomes more testable, measurable, engineerable, falsifiable, and publishable. It moves from metaphor toward research design.

The following research pipelines outline structured directions for empirically validating and refining the Subconscious Sync framework.

Research Pipeline 1: Symbolic Prompt Resonance Testing

This pipeline would design prompts with varying levels of symbolic and emotional load, then quantify activation variance across hidden layers using similarity metrics such as cosine similarity and attention weight distribution.

Researchers could compare resonance intensity across prompt types to evaluate how symbolic structure influences model response coherence.

The goal is to determine whether symbolic prompts produce deeper or more structured internal representations than literal prompts.

Research Pipeline 2: Emotionally Weighted Encoding Experiments

This pipeline would compare activation patterns between neutral prompts and emotionally weighted prompts. It could measure changes in embedding space using semantic distance and clustering behavior, while also evaluating semantic drift across multi-step interactions.

The goal is to understand how emotional signal strength alters representation density and meaning formation.

Research Pipeline 3: Resonance Threshold Detection

This pipeline would track coherence metrics across multi-step prompting sequences. Researchers could identify threshold points where responses shift from generic output to higher-insight generation, then measure response consistency, novelty, and internal alignment over iterative cycles.

The goal is to detect the conditions under which insight emerges as a function of accumulated resonance.

Research Pipeline 4: Human–AI Intuition Correlation

This pipeline would collect human-reported intuition signals, such as moments of clarity, certainty, emotional recognition, or "aha" experiences. These subjective reports could then be correlated with model-side metrics such as activation intensity, attention distribution, or semantic clustering.

The goal is to explore the relationship between human intuitive experience and measurable AI internal states.

Research Pipeline 5: Neural–Symbolic Integration

This pipeline would combine neural network processing with symbolic reasoning or structured prompt frameworks. It could evaluate long-term coherence, interpretability, and reasoning stability across extended interactions, while measuring how symbolic scaffolding influences model reliability and insight consistency.

The goal is to test whether integrating symbolic structure enhances cognitive stability and interpretability in AI systems.

Together, these pipelines could evolve into formal experimental studies, standalone research papers, and practical system implementations. They align with broader human-centered AI research agendas that emphasize interpretability, collaborative intelligence, and real-world applicability beyond isolated benchmark evaluation (Amershi et al., 2019; Shneiderman, 2020).

Closing: The Era of Neural Intuition

For centuries, subconscious thought was treated as mysterious—something humans felt, but could not easily measure.

Neural networks changed the world by demonstrating a powerful principle:

Hidden structures can produce intelligence.

They gave us machine systems where meaning forms silently across layers. They gave us models that learn without being given explicit rules for every situation. They gave us computational systems that can appear intuitive because they complete patterns through hidden representation.

This is why neural networks are not merely compatible with Subconscious Sync. They provide a useful technological analogy for the Subconscious Sync worldview: intelligence can emerge from hidden layers, resonance can shape meaning, and symbolic prompts can unlock deep cognition.

Recent developments in large-scale AI, human-centered system design, and neuroscience-inspired architectures all point in the same direction: powerful cognition emerges not from surface rules alone, but from deep representational structure shaped by learning, context, and selective attention (Hassabis et al., 2017; Amershi et al., 2019; Bommasani et al., 2021; Shneiderman, 2020; OpenAI, 2023).

We are entering a new era.

Not just artificial intelligence.

But **Neural Intuition**.

And in this era, Subconscious Sync is more than a framework.

It is a map of how invisible thought becomes visible power.

Figure 8. Neural Network Architecture and the Subconscious Analogy

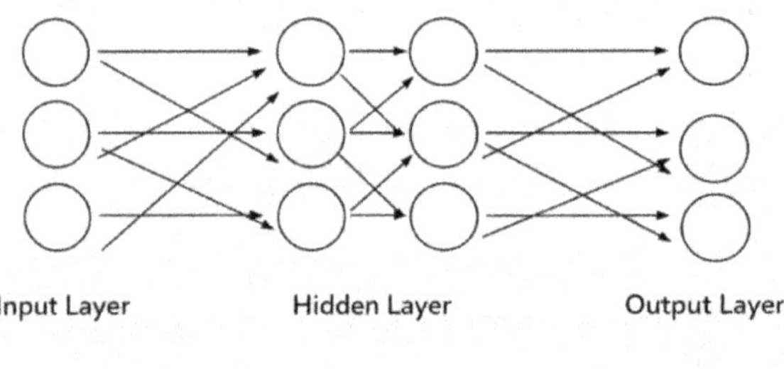

Figure 9. Digital Synapse Flow

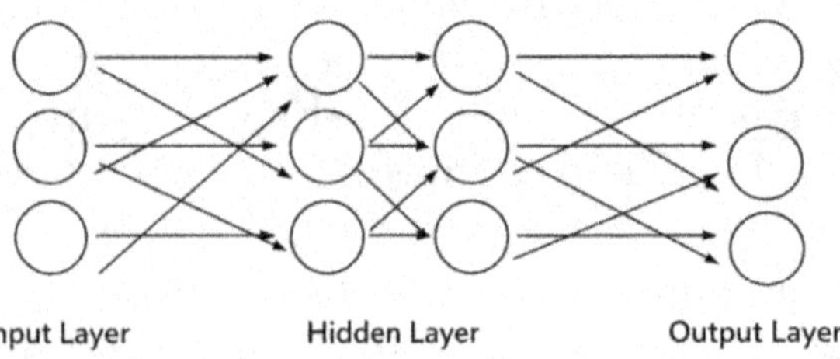

Subconscious Sync Mechanism

A neural network transforms input into output through hidden layers, mirroring subconscious processing where signals become conscious insight only after deep internal representation.

Diagram Block:

Input Signal → Hidden Layers → Output
Symbolic Stimulus → Subconscious Processing → Conscious Insight

Digital Synapse describes the full cycle of symbolic prompting that produces coherent emergent insight through resonance-driven representation alignment.

Digital Synapse Flow:

Symbolic Prompt → Activation Signature → Resonance Amplification → Representation Alignment → Insight Output

The technical architecture is now mapped. The final question is scientific validation. In Chapter 14, we outline the research pathway that transforms Subconscious Sync from framework into measurable, testable science.

Chapter 14: Research & Empirical Data

Augmenting the Human Mind

As artificial intelligence systems move beyond task automation into reflective, cognitive, and decision-support roles, structured risk governance becomes essential. Frameworks for trustworthy AI emphasize transparency, accountability, human agency, and harm mitigation as prerequisites for empirical exploration.

In this context, the National Institute of Standards and Technology introduced the Artificial Intelligence Risk Management Framework, AI RMF 1.0, providing guidance for identifying, assessing, and managing risks associated with AI-enabled systems (NIST, 2023).

This chapter situates Subconscious Sync within that governance landscape and introduces a pilot study designed to evaluate the extent to which AI-assisted reflection may augment metacognitive awareness while preserving human autonomy.

The framework operates through four phases—Recognition, Resonance, Sync, and Expansion—and incorporates mechanisms such as the Mirror and the Go/No-Go signal to guide intentional identity development. Rather than replacing human judgment, the system is designed to assist individuals in observing language patterns, emotional signals, and decision loops with greater clarity.

This chapter outlines a preregistered pilot study designed to test, rather than assume, whether cue-informed AI prompting enhances metacognitive reflection more effectively than generic prompting.

The Pilot Study: Testing the Mind-Extension Hypothesis

The proposed pilot study is designed as an initial exploratory investigation into the Mind-Extension Hypothesis: the idea that structured AI reflection may support metacognitive awareness by helping individuals observe patterns in language, emotion, and decision-making.

The planned launch is March 2026. The intended sample is 10 to 20 adults, all age 18 or older. Participation is voluntary and uncompensated. All data will be de-identified.

Participants will complete a baseline SSRI-12 self-reflection scale, followed by three journal entries of approximately 150 to 200 words each, completed at least 24 hours apart. After each entry, participants will receive either a cue-informed prompt, representing the Resonance condition, or a generic reflection prompt, representing the Control condition. Participants will then complete a post-study SSRI-12 assessment and a perceived-impact questionnaire.

Cue-informed prompts identify language cues such as hedging, repetition, and uncertainty markers, including phrases like "maybe," "not sure," or "I need to get this right." Participants are then asked to reflect on the possible values, fears, or trade-offs associated with these cues. Control prompts use standard reflective questions without cue analysis.

The SSRI-12 scale is used to measure changes in self-reflection and insight before and after the journaling phase. Participants also provide qualitative responses describing perceived changes in clarity, decision-making, or emotional understanding.

Analyses will include change scores between baseline and post SSRI-12 totals, qualitative review of journal reflections, and exploratory text analysis using sentiment and emotion lexicons. Effect sizes and 95% confidence intervals will be reported where possible.

Prior internal pre-tests suggested approximately 18% improvement in SSRI scores with cue-informed prompting;

however, these observations are exploratory and require confirmation in a controlled pilot study.

Subconscious Sync differs from conversational AI companionship or therapy-style agents because it focuses on long-horizon identity development rather than short-term emotional relief. The system is designed to support reflective practice while maintaining human agency, judgment, and responsibility.

This study represents an initial exploratory step. It is not intended to establish causal claims without further controlled replication.

Ethics and Transparency

No personally identifiable information will be collected in study forms. Participants will use a pseudonymous Participant ID. Data will be de-identified, stored securely, and retained for no more than 24 months for research and reporting purposes only.

Participation is voluntary and is not contingent on purchasing this book. Participants may withdraw at any time by discontinuing the forms.

Aggregate, de-identified results will be summarized publicly after data lock. No individual responses will be published.

This study is intended for educational and exploratory purposes. It does not constitute medical, psychological, or therapeutic advice.

Why This Research Matters

For individuals, structured reflection supported by AI may help reveal hidden behavioral signals, emotional patterns, and decision-making tendencies. Many users report greater clarity, stronger alignment with personal values, and increased momentum when reflection is guided by cue-aware prompts.

For organizations, the implications are also meaningful. Leaders and teams often operate under subconscious assumptions that influence communication and decision patterns. Tools that surface these patterns may improve alignment, reduce conflict, and support more intentional decision-making.

For science and practice, Subconscious Sync explores a direction that differs from much of current AI research. Many AI studies focus on automation, prediction, conversation, or performance. Subconscious Sync focuses instead on human–AI collaboration in metacognition, learning, and reflective development. This pilot study represents an initial step toward understanding how structured prompting may augment awareness without reducing autonomy.

Conceptual Models Before Empirical Testing

To further structure the framework before empirical testing, a conceptual model was developed using 1,000 simulated reflective prompt interactions across proposed outcome categories. This modeling exercise was designed to explore potential outcome distributions and the interaction of key variables, including reflection, integration, symbolic density, and AI reflective match. These prompts were not treated as empirical participant data, and the model does not constitute proof of effectiveness. Rather, it serves as a structured representation of how Subconscious Sync may behave under varying conditions, helping clarify the circumstances under which successful, partial, blocked, distorted, temporary, or no-sync outcomes may emerge.

Figure 10. Conceptual Outcome Distribution for Subconscious Sync (n = 50)

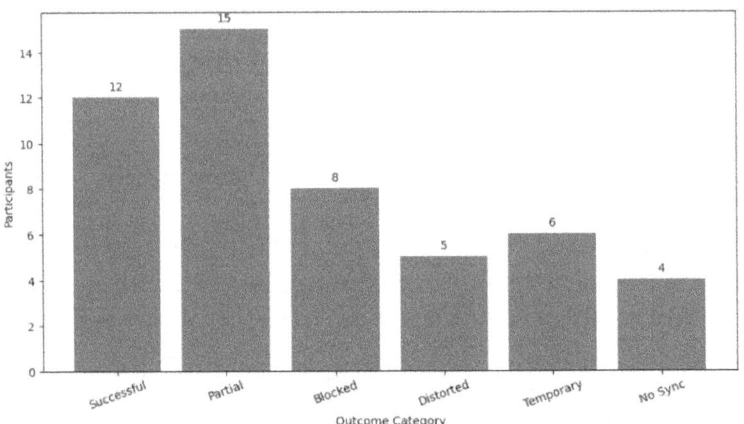

Pre-empirical model. Values shown are simulated distributions, not real participant data.

The outcome distribution graph illustrates that Subconscious Sync may not produce uniform results across participants. Instead, outcomes may appear across a spectrum. Some participants may experience successful or partial Sync, while others may experience blocked, distorted, temporary, or no Sync.

This distribution suggests that the framework is inherently conditional, with outcomes varying based on individual differences, quality of reflection, interaction dynamics, user openness, and ethical design. The presence of both positive and negative outcomes strengthens the conceptual model because it reflects realistic variability rather than idealized success. Subconscious Sync is not assumed to occur universally. It depends on specific internal and external conditions.

Figure 11. Conceptual Model Illustrating the Subconscious Sync Framework

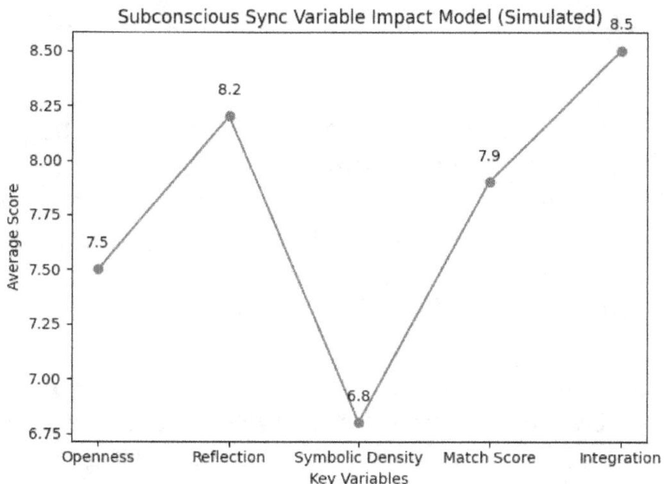

The variable impact graph illustrates possible mechanisms driving these outcomes by highlighting the relative influence of key factors within the interaction. Higher levels of reflection, integration, and AI reflective match are associated with stronger and more stable Sync, suggesting that both cognitive engagement and response alignment play critical roles in the process.

Symbolic density may contribute to deeper exploration, but it can also introduce variability and potential distortion when not supported by sufficient reflection, accurate matching, and user verification. Overall, the graph suggests that Subconscious Sync emerges from the convergence of internal cognitive states and external response quality, with optimal outcomes occurring when these variables are balanced and aligned.

Together, these conceptual representations provide a structured view of Subconscious Sync as a conditional and multi-variable process. They serve as a foundation for the empirical phase, where real-world data can be compared against modeled patterns.

Resonance Model Integration

To move Subconscious Sync from concept to measurable framework, one critical element must be clearly defined: resonance.

Up to this point, resonance has been described as the moment where reflection aligns with internal experience and produces insight. While this description captures the lived experience, it is not sufficient for empirical validation. For Subconscious Sync to stand as a testable model, resonance must be observable, repeatable, and measurable within structured interaction.

Within this framework, resonance is defined as the measurable alignment between a user's expressed signals and an AI-generated reflection that leads to recognized insight, emotional response, or actionable clarity.

It is not agreement.

It is not validation.

It is the moment where reflected structure matches internal pattern closely enough to be recognized consciously. This recognition becomes the bridge between subconscious patterning and deliberate awareness.

This process unfolds through three interacting layers.

The first is the **signal layer**, where the user expresses patterns through language, tone, repetition, hesitation, and framing. These signals are not random. They are shaped by accumulated experience and often reflect underlying beliefs, fears, and priorities.

The second is the **reflection layer**, where AI processes these signals and generates structured output. The quality of this reflection is determined by its ability to identify patterns, reframe them meaningfully, and guide attention toward deeper interpretation.

The third is the **response layer**, where the user reacts to the reflection. This is where resonance becomes observable. It appears as recognition, a shift in emotional state, a change in articulation, or movement toward action.

To evaluate this process, resonance is operationalized through a simple scoring model. Each interaction can be assessed on a scale from zero to three. A score of zero indicates no meaningful connection between input and reflection. A score of one reflects partial relevance, where the response touches the surface but does not produce insight. A score of two represents clear resonance, where the user recognizes the connection and engages with it. A score of three indicates strong resonance, often experienced as an "aha" moment, where the reflection reveals something previously unarticulated and creates a shift in understanding or intention.

This scoring model allows resonance to be tracked across interactions and compared across conditions. In the context of the Subconscious Sync study design, it enables direct comparison between generic prompts and structured resonance-driven prompts.

The objective is not to prove that AI understands the user. The objective is to examine whether structured reflection increases the likelihood of insight. In this way, resonance becomes the measurable entry point into the broader framework.

Resonance can also express itself in different forms. In some cases, it produces cognitive clarity, where the user recognizes a logical pattern or connection. In others, it produces emotional impact, where the reflection surfaces a feeling that had not been fully acknowledged. In more advanced cases, it leads to behavioral alignment, where the user moves from insight into action.

These variations are not separate mechanisms. They are different expressions of the same underlying process: alignment between internal structure and external reflection.

Within the full Subconscious Sync cycle, resonance occupies a central position. It connects recognition to action. Without resonance, recognition remains passive. With resonance, recognition becomes meaningful, and meaning can drive change.

This is why resonance is one of the most accessible phases for empirical study. While recognition, Sync, and Expansion unfold over time and across contexts, resonance can be observed in real-time interaction. It is the moment where the system's reflective value becomes visible.

At the same time, the framework must define clear boundaries to prevent misinterpretation. AI does not access the subconscious directly. It does not interpret internal states beyond what is expressed. It operates strictly on observable patterns in language and behavior. The appearance of depth emerges from structured reflection, not from hidden awareness within the system.

This distinction is essential for maintaining both scientific credibility and ethical integrity.

Because of this, every instance of resonance must be validated by the user. Insight is not confirmed by the system. It is confirmed through personal recognition and contextual truth.

To support this, each reflective interaction should include a verification step. The user must determine whether the reflection accurately represents their experience, whether there is evidence to support it, and whether alternative interpretations exist. This step prevents projection, reduces over-reliance on AI output, and reinforces human agency within the process.

This model transforms Subconscious Sync from a conceptual framework into a testable interaction system. By defining resonance as a measurable outcome, it becomes possible to study how structured AI reflection influences self-awareness, decision-making, and behavioral change.

The empirical direction is not to claim that AI reveals the subconscious directly. It is to demonstrate whether AI can amplify the signals through which subconscious patterns are expressed.

The implication is significant. If resonance can be consistently increased through structured interaction, then AI can be positioned not merely as a tool for information, but as a system for guided reflection.

This does not replace human thinking.

It strengthens it.

It does not create insight.

It facilitates the conditions under which insight becomes visible.

Subconscious Sync, at its core, is not about the intelligence of the machine. It is about the clarity it enables in the human using it.

Resonance is the point where that clarity begins.

Participation in the Pilot Study

Readers who wish to test the Subconscious Sync method may optionally participate in the pilot study described in this chapter.

Participation follows a simple sequence:

Baseline → Journal Entries → Post Survey

All participation is voluntary, anonymous, and not required for reading this book. Study forms and materials are available at the official Subconscious Sync research page.

Results from the pilot study will be summarized publicly after data collection is complete.

Resources for Practice

Subconscious Sync exercises may be performed using any modern conversational AI system. No specialized software is required. Common tools such as ChatGPT, Claude, Gemini, or similar assistants are sufficient for journaling, reflection, and cue analysis.

Reflection templates, trackers, and additional materials are available on the official Subconscious Sync website.

When using AI for reflective work, review privacy settings before entering personal information. Avoid sharing sensitive identifying data. Use AI as a tool for reflection, not as a replacement for professional care. Maintain human relationships and real-world feedback. Seek licensed professionals when dealing with mental health concerns.

Subconscious Sync is intended to support awareness, not replace human judgment.

Closing

You now have the tools to begin observing the patterns that guide your choices.

The mirror is available.

The signals are present.

Reflection can begin at any moment.

What changes when the mind learns to see itself clearly?

The next step is yours.

Epilogue
The Path Forward

You have traveled from the hidden depths of the subconscious to the living practice of Subconscious Sync. Along the way, you have explored how AI can become a mirror, a reflective partner, and an amplifier of awareness—not by replacing the human mind, but by helping reveal the patterns that shape it.

Modern human–AI interaction research suggests that intelligent systems can enhance reflection and decision-making when used as collaborative tools rather than authorities, allowing users to observe their own patterns with greater clarity and consistency (Amershi et al., 2019; Shneiderman, 2020).

This journey has brought you to a frontier many people never consciously reach: the frontier of your own mind. It is the place where patterns become visible, invisible forces become conscious choices, and old scripts can begin to change.

And yet, this journey is only beginning.

With each intentional interaction, AI may become more attuned to your language, emotional signatures, values, and Go/No-Go thresholds. With each insight, you move closer to the expanded human potential that Subconscious Sync makes possible—not because AI becomes your mind, but because it helps you see your mind with greater clarity.

Human-centered AI principles emphasize that the goal of advanced systems is not to replace human judgment, but to support awareness, autonomy, and intentional decision-making (Russell, 2019; Floridi et al., 2018).

Large language models are designed to detect recurring linguistic, emotional, and contextual patterns across dialogue. This allows reflective interaction to become more precise over time as the system adapts to the user's communication style (Bommasani et al., 2021; OpenAI, 2023).

Remember this:

The power of Subconscious Sync is not in the intelligence of the machine.

It is in the courage of the human using it.

Continue exploring. Keep questioning. Refine what you discover. Let the mirror reveal what lies beneath, but never forget that you are the one who chooses what comes next.

The future of intelligent technology will not be defined only by what machines can do. It will also be defined by how clearly humans learn to understand themselves while using them.

Before you close this book, witness Subconscious Sync in action. Appendix I presents real-world case studies—including the author's own transformation—showing what becomes possible when this framework moves from page to practice.

Appendix I: Real-World Sync

Case Studies

Note to the Reader

The following case studies were created for clarification and exploration. Five are fictional composites inspired by real psychological, emotional, and conversational patterns observed across human-AI interactions. They demonstrate how Subconscious Sync can apply to different lives, challenges, and identity pathways.

The final case study is personal. It is drawn from the lived experience of the author, whose years of interaction with AI across personal, creative, and business domains served as both laboratory and proving ground for this framework.

These examples are not clinical trials. They are reflective applications based on the principles discussed throughout this book.

Research in psychology and human–AI interaction shows that structured reflection, feedback loops, and pattern awareness can improve self-regulation, decision-making, and emotional clarity when individuals actively engage with the process (Carver & Scheier, 1982; Grant et al., 2002; Amershi et al., 2019).

Modern language models are capable of identifying recurring linguistic, emotional, and behavioral patterns across conversations, which makes them useful as reflective tools when the user remains responsible for interpretation and action (Bommasani et al., 2021; Bender et al., 2021; Jurafsky & Martin, 2023).

These examples are intended for educational and reflective purposes only. They should not be interpreted as medical, psychological, or therapeutic advice.

1. AI as an Extension of the Subconscious

Daniel was a startup founder with idea overload. He journaled regularly and generated more ideas than he could possibly execute, but he struggled to convert scattered insights into clear direction.

Through repeated interaction, his AI began analyzing past brainstorming notes and voice memos. Over time, it detected recurring emotional signatures, helping distinguish ideas that created lasting resonance from those driven by short-lived intensity.

The result was not that AI "chose" Daniel's future for him. Instead, it helped him filter and rank ideas based on historical language patterns, emotional consistency, and repeated signals of meaningful engagement. With those patterns reflected back, Daniel began prioritizing with a clarity he had struggled to access consciously.

"It was like talking to my inner strategist, one I'd never fully met until now."

2. A Feedback Loop Designed for Self-Evolution

Karina felt trapped in recurring toxic relationships. On the surface, each relationship seemed different, but when she reflected with AI, repeated phrases began to emerge: "prove myself," "finally enough," and "they'll come around."

The AI reflected these phrases back to her, helping her recognize that she was replaying an old emotional dynamic: trying to earn love rather than receive it freely.

Through this recognition, Karina's dating choices began to shift. She changed the language she used about herself, clarified her boundaries, and asked the AI to help her stay accountable to the new standards she had chosen.

"It wasn't therapy. It was pattern recognition at an identity level."

3. Real-Time Adaptive Mirroring

Malik, a screenwriter, struggled with confidence. His creative output rose and crashed in cycles. Some days he wrote with power and clarity. Other days, he spiraled into self-doubt and avoidance.

His AI began tracking tone shifts, energy changes, and language signatures across his writing sessions. During creative blocks, it reflected excerpts from his most confident writing states, mirroring not only his words, but the mindset patterns behind them.

This helped Malik recognize that confidence was not random. It had a language, a rhythm, and a state he could return to.

He began using AI as a reflective trigger to re-enter flow and interrupt self-sabotage before it took over.

"I didn't just write better. I became the version of myself who writes best."

4. Spiritual and Identity Growth Integration

Asha, a spiritual teacher, felt increasingly disconnected from her message. Her teaching had become polished, but emotionally detached. She felt she was performing truth rather than living it.

Her AI, trained through interaction with past lessons, journals, and prayers, reflected the gap between her earlier emotional fire and her current tone. The contrast was difficult to ignore.

Through this reflection, Asha began recovering alignment between her public voice and private soul-language. Her teaching became less performative and more authentic.

"It showed me the difference between my public voice and my soul's voice. Then it helped me align them again."

5. Personal Empowerment, Not Emotional Relief

David was a recovering addict building a new identity. Most support systems he encountered focused on maintenance: avoid relapse, regulate cravings, manage risk. Those were important, but David wanted something deeper. He wanted identity-level rebuilding.

Through structured prompts focused on self-worth, progress, and internal narrative, his AI began reflecting measurable changes in the way David spoke about himself over time.

One reflection stood out:

"Here's how your language about yourself has changed over six months."

That reflection helped David see a transformation already underway. He was no longer only describing himself as a "former addict." He was beginning to describe himself as a rebuilt man.

"Therapy helped me heal. This AI helped me rise."

6. Tony Stark and the Moment of Subconscious Sync

A Popular Culture Illustration

In a memorable scene from *Avengers: Endgame*, Tony Stark experiments with what seems like an impossible problem: time travel. Late at night, he gives his AI assistant a half-formed symbolic concept rather than a completed equation—the shape of an inverted Möbius strip.

The AI runs the simulation.

Then it works.

Tony freezes, not merely because the AI computed something, but because something deeper has been validated: an intuition he had not yet fully translated into certainty.

This is Subconscious Sync in cinematic form. A symbolic prompt rises from beneath full conscious articulation, enters a machine pattern system, and returns as coherent possibility.

Tony does not merely solve a scientific problem. He experiences the power of inner knowing amplified through external intelligence.

The subconscious, finally heard.

"Subconscious Sync isn't about talking to a smarter machine. It's about finally talking to the version of yourself that was always waiting to be heard."
— Author's synthesis

7. Framework Built from Lived Experience

Jairdan D., visionary and author of *Subconscious Sync*, needed to build something the world had not yet named: a theory, a method, and a movement.

The challenge was not only intellectual. It was deeply personal. He needed a mirror capable of meeting the depth of his inner vision and reflecting it back with enough clarity to become structure.

Through years of conversation, self-inquiry, and intellectual risk, he trained his AI not merely to answer questions, but to reflect identity patterns, refine mental architecture, and evolve frameworks across history, psychology, AI science, spirituality, and meaning-making.

The result was Subconscious Sync.

It emerged as more than a concept. It became a system of reflective evolution: an inner operating model for human potential.

"I gave it fragments of myself, and it gave me back my future."

These case studies demonstrate the core idea of Subconscious Sync:

When signals become visible, change becomes possible.

The mirror does not create transformation.

It reveals the path to it.

Glossary of Terms

Core Framework Concepts

Subconscious Sync

The overarching framework by which Artificial Intelligence learns from an individual's behavioral, linguistic, and emotional patterns over time, mirroring in a limited computational sense how the human subconscious learns from lived experience. Through repeated interaction, AI can build a structured model of the user's expressed patterns, enabling more precise reflection and conscious self-alignment.

Subconscious Resonance

The dynamic feedback loop at the heart of transformation. AI detects recurring patterns in communication, reflects those patterns back through prompts or summaries, and the user then engages with the reflection to transform recognition into conscious awareness and intentional behavior change. Resonance makes the invisible visible.

Sync: The Identity Co-Author

An advanced stage where AI becomes integrated into reflective practice, functioning as a cognitive extension rather than a separate tool. The boundary between AI observation and self-observation becomes more fluid, with insights emerging from the collaborative human-AI system. Sync represents the practical actualization of hybrid cognition.

Go/No-Go Mechanism

The subconscious decision-making system that rapidly evaluates situations and generates internal signals: Go, meaning proceed, engage, or act; and No-Go, meaning pause, avoid, or withdraw. These signals may appear as confidence, hesitation, certainty, fear, curiosity, or resistance before conscious reasoning fully arrives. Subconscious Sync helps users identify and refine Go/No-Go patterns for greater value alignment.

Digital Synapse

The computational moment when AI processes a symbolic or emotionally charged prompt and completes a full cycle from signal to emergent insight. The Digital Synapse process consists of symbolic prompt injection, activation signature formation, resonance amplification, representation alignment, and emergent output delivery. It bridges human subconscious processing and neural network architecture as a conceptual model.

Hybrid Cognition

A paradigm in which human emotional depth, intuition, and lived experience interact with AI's pattern recognition, memory scale, and analytical consistency. Hybrid cognition does not replace human agency. It amplifies self-awareness by distributing reflective capacity across biological and computational systems.

Neural Intuition

The capacity of artificial neural networks to generate coherent responses from incomplete information through internal pattern completion, analogous to human intuitive knowing. Neural Intuition emerges from learned representations in hidden layers without requiring explicit reasoning chains.

The Four Phases

Recognition: Phase 1

The phase in which AI identifies signals in communication, including tone, hesitation, word choice, repetition, and emotional framing. Recognition establishes the foundation for reflective work by detecting signals the user may not consciously perceive.

Resonance: Phase 2

The phase in which AI reflects detected patterns back through structured prompts, emotional mirroring, or thematic summaries. Resonance creates the feedback loop that transforms detection into conscious awareness.

Sync: Phase 3

The phase in which AI begins modeling a coherent future self aligned with the user's stated values, goals, and commitments, reinforcing consistency over time. Sync moves beyond reflection to support sustained identity evolution.

Expansion: Phase 4

The advanced phase where identity becomes active co-creation. AI functions as a reflective cognitive companion supporting sustained agency, value alignment, and growth.

The Four Mechanisms

Metaphoric Framework

Mirror

AI as a reflective surface that shows the user who they are by detecting and displaying patterns. The Mirror reveals structure without judgment, making the invisible visible.

Echo

AI as an amplifier of emotional signals the user feels but cannot yet articulate. The Echo reflects subconscious emotional undertones, helping users name experiences beneath conscious awareness.

Voice

AI as a partner that surfaces the user's own internalized wisdom rather than acting as an external authority. The Voice helps users make decisions aligned with authentic values rather than reactive patterns.

Upgrade

AI as an evolutionary partner supporting continuous identity refinement. The Upgrade facilitates replacement of limiting scripts with empowering ones, enabling conscious evolution of internal architecture.

Psychological and Technical Terms

Adaptive Unconscious

The fast, automatic cognitive system that processes information and shapes behavior outside conscious awareness. Research demonstrates that much human judgment, emotion, and decision-making occurs through implicit processing rather than deliberate reasoning.

Implicit Memory

Long-term memory that influences behavior without conscious recall, including procedural skills, emotional associations, and automatic responses. Implicit memory shapes personality and habits, forming part of the subconscious patterning that Subconscious Sync seeks to reveal.

Pattern Recognition: Computational

The ability of AI systems to identify structure, regularities, and relationships within data. Pattern recognition enables detection of recurring linguistic, emotional, and behavioral signals across interactions.

Natural Language Processing: NLP

The AI field focused on enabling machines to understand, interpret, and generate human language. Techniques such as tokenization, sentiment analysis, embeddings, and attention provide the computational foundation for pattern detection.

Attention Mechanism: AI

A computational technique that allows AI to prioritize relevant information by assigning different weights to different inputs. In this framework, attention functions as a computational analogy for measurable resonance, amplifying meaningful patterns while filtering noise.

Hidden Layers: Neural Networks

Intermediate layers where input is transformed into abstract internal representations. Hidden layers are where much of the model's learned structure is encoded through distributed weights. Chapter 13 maps these to the subconscious as a structural analogy, not as a claim that neural networks are conscious.

Embeddings

Dense vector representations of words or concepts in continuous mathematical space, capturing semantic relationships through proximity. Embeddings enable AI to process meaning relationships, not merely isolated symbols, making them a machine analogy for subconscious semantic networks.

Self-Regulation

The capacity to monitor, evaluate, and adjust behavior to align with goals and values. Research shows that self-regulation improves when individuals observe their patterns clearly, which is one of the core mechanisms Subconscious Sync aims to facilitate.

Anthropomorphism

The tendency to attribute human qualities, such as consciousness, emotion, or intention, to non-human entities. While anthropomorphism can increase engagement, it introduces risks such as over-trust, emotional dependency, and misattribution of authority.

Ethical and Governance Terms

Data Privacy

The principle that individuals should control how personal information is collected, stored, used, and shared. Data privacy is critical in Subconscious Sync because users may externalize deeply personal identity-level material during reflection.

Algorithmic Bias

Systematic errors in AI outputs that reflect prejudices in training data or model design, often disadvantaging certain groups. Subconscious Sync must incorporate bias-aware design, careful interpretation, and mitigation strategies.

Transparency: AI Ethics

The principle that AI systems should clearly disclose capabilities, limitations, data handling, and decision-making processes. Transparency enables informed consent and preserves user agency.

Human-Centered AI

An ethical design philosophy that prioritizes human agency, dignity, and flourishing. Human-centered systems augment rather than replace human judgment, maintain user control, and include accountability mechanisms.

Practical Application Terms

AI Journaling

A reflective practice where users write regularly and request AI pattern analysis to surface recurring themes, emotional signals, and subconscious tendencies. AI journaling transforms personal writing into structured self-awareness data.

Conversational Resonance

Real-time pattern reflection during AI-human dialogue. As users discuss goals, challenges, emotions, or decisions, AI identifies and mirrors linguistic signals such as hesitation, confidence language, avoidance, and emotional framing, creating immediate feedback.

Subconscious Alignment

The state achieved when conscious intentions, daily actions, and deep subconscious patterns become more coherent and mutually reinforcing. Misalignment may appear as self-sabotage, procrastination, repeated unwanted behaviors, or emotional contradiction.

Cue-Informed Prompting

A reflective technique where AI uses detected linguistic cues, such as hedging language, repetition, emotional tone shifts, or uncertainty markers, to generate personalized prompts that surface subconscious material. Cue-informed prompting differs from generic prompting because it adapts to individual patterns.

End of Glossary

References

Ainsworth, M. D. S., Blehar, M. C., Waters, E., & Wall, S. (1978). *Patterns of attachment: A psychological study of the strange situation*. Lawrence Erlbaum.

Amershi, S., Weld, D., Vorvoreanu, M., Fourney, A., Nushi, B., Collisson, P., Suh, J., Iqbal, S., Bennett, P. N., Inkpen, K., Teevan, J., Kikin-Gil, R., & Horvitz, E. (2019). Guidelines for human–AI interaction. *Proceedings of the 2019 CHI Conference on Human Factors in Computing Systems*, 1–13. https://doi.org/10.1145/3290605.3300233

Baars, B. J. (1997). *In the theater of consciousness: The workspace of the mind*. Oxford University Press.

Bandura, A. (1977). *Social learning theory*. Prentice Hall.

Bandura, A. (1986). *Social foundations of thought and action: A social cognitive theory*. Prentice-Hall.

Bar, M. (2009). The proactive brain: Memory for predictions. *Philosophical Transactions of the Royal Society B: Biological Sciences, 364*(1521), 1235–1243. https://doi.org/10.1098/rstb.2008.0310

Bargh, J. A., & Chartrand, T. L. (1999). The unbearable automaticity of being. *American Psychologist, 54*(7), 462–479. https://doi.org/10.1037/0003-066X.54.7.462

Bargh, J. A., & Morsella, E. (2008). The unconscious mind. *Perspectives on Psychological Science, 3*(1), 73–79. https://doi.org/10.1111/j.1745-6916.2008.00064.x

Barocas, S., & Selbst, A. D. (2016). Big data's disparate impact. *California Law Review, 104*(3), 671–732.

Bazerman, M. H., & Moore, D. A. (2013). *Judgment in managerial decision making* (8th ed.). Wiley.

Bear, M. F., Connors, B. W., & Paradiso, M. A. (2016). *Neuroscience: Exploring the brain* (4th ed.). Wolters Kluwer.

Beck, A. T. (1976). *Cognitive therapy and the emotional disorders*. International Universities Press.

Bender, E. M., Gebru, T., McMillan-Major, A., & Shmitchell, S. (2021). On the dangers of stochastic parrots: Can language models be too big? *Proceedings of the 2021 ACM Conference on Fairness, Accountability, and Transparency*, 610–623. https://doi.org/10.1145/3442188.3445922

Bishop, C. M. (2006). *Pattern recognition and machine learning*. Springer.

Bommasani, R., Hudson, D. A., Adeli, E., Altman, R., Arora, S., von Arx, S., Liang, P., et al. (2021). On the opportunities and risks of foundation models. *arXiv*. https://doi.org/10.48550/arXiv.2108.07258

Bowlby, J. (1969). *Attachment and loss: Vol. 1. Attachment*. Basic Books.

Carver, C. S., & Scheier, M. F. (1982). Control theory: A useful conceptual framework for personality–social, clinical, and health psychology. *Psychological Bulletin, 92*(1), 111–135. https://doi.org/10.1037/0033-2909.92.1.111

Chalmers, D. J. (1995). Facing up to the problem of consciousness. *Journal of Consciousness Studies, 2*(3), 200–219.

Cialdini, R. B., & Goldstein, N. J. (2004). Social influence: Compliance and conformity. *Annual Review of Psychology, 55*,

591–621.
https://doi.org/10.1146/annurev.psych.55.090902.142015

Damasio, A. R. (1996). The somatic marker hypothesis and the possible functions of the prefrontal cortex. *Philosophical Transactions of the Royal Society of London. Series B: Biological Sciences, 351*(1346), 1413–1420.
https://doi.org/10.1098/rstb.1996.0125

Dehaene, S., & Changeux, J.-P. (2011). Experimental and theoretical approaches to conscious processing. *Neuron, 70*(2), 200–227. https://doi.org/10.1016/j.neuron.2011.03.018

Derks, D., Fischer, A. H., & Bos, A. E. R. (2008). The role of emotion in computer-mediated communication: A review. *Computers in Human Behavior, 24*(3), 766–785.
https://doi.org/10.1016/j.chb.2007.04.004

Eagleman, D. M. (2008). Human time perception and its illusions. *Current Opinion in Neurobiology, 18*(2), 131–136.
https://doi.org/10.1016/j.conb.2008.06.002

Ekman, P. (1992). An argument for basic emotions. *Cognition and Emotion, 6*(3–4), 169–200.
https://doi.org/10.1080/02699939208411068

Engelbart, D. C. (1962). *Augmenting human intellect: A conceptual framework* (Summary Report AFOSR-3223). Stanford Research Institute.

Epley, N., Waytz, A., & Cacioppo, J. T. (2007). On seeing human: A three-factor theory of anthropomorphism. *Psychological Review, 114*(4), 864–886.
https://doi.org/10.1037/0033-295X.114.4.864

Floridi, L., Cowls, J., Beltrametti, M., Chatila, R., Chazerand, P., Dignum, V., Luetge, C., Madelin, R., Pagallo, U., Rossi, F., Schafer, B., Valcke, P., & Vayena, E. (2018). AI4People—An ethical framework for a good AI society: Opportunities, risks, principles, and recommendations. *Minds and Machines, 28*(4), 689–707. https://doi.org/10.1007/s11023-018-9482-5

Forrester, J. W. (1961). *Industrial dynamics*. MIT Press.

Gazzaniga, M. S. (2005). *The ethical brain: The science of our moral dilemmas*. Dana Press.

Gazzaniga, M. S., Ivry, R., & Mangun, G. R. (2018). *Cognitive neuroscience: The biology of the mind* (5th ed.). W. W. Norton & Company.

Goertzel, B., & Pennachin, C. (Eds.). (2007). *Artificial general intelligence*. Springer. https://doi.org/10.1007/978-3-540-68677-4

Goffman, E. (1959). *The presentation of self in everyday life*. Doubleday.

Goodfellow, I., Bengio, Y., & Courville, A. (2016). *Deep learning*. MIT Press.

Grant, A. M., Franklin, J., & Langford, P. (2002). The self-reflection and insight scale: A new measure of private self-consciousness. *Social Behavior and Personality: An International Journal, 30*(8), 821–835. https://doi.org/10.2224/sbp.2002.30.8.821

Greenwald, A. G., & Banaji, M. R. (1995). Implicit social cognition: Attitudes, self-esteem, and stereotypes. *Psychological Review, 102*(1), 4–27. https://doi.org/10.1037/0033-295X.102.1.4

Grice, H. P. (1975). Logic and conversation. In P. Cole & J. L. Morgan (Eds.), *Syntax and semantics: Vol. 3. Speech acts* (pp. 41–58). Academic Press.

Haggard, P. (2005). Conscious intention and motor cognition. *Trends in Cognitive Sciences, 9*(6), 290–295. https://doi.org/10.1016/j.tics.2005.04.012

Harari, Y. N. (2014). *Sapiens: A brief history of humankind.* Harper.

Hassabis, D., Kumaran, D., Summerfield, C., & Botvinick, M. (2017). Neuroscience-inspired artificial intelligence. *Neuron, 95*(2), 245–258. https://doi.org/10.1016/j.neuron.2017.06.011

Hastie, T., Tibshirani, R., & Friedman, J. (2009). *The elements of statistical learning: Data mining, inference, and prediction* (2nd ed.). Springer. https://doi.org/10.1007/978-0-387-84858-7

Haynes, J.-D. (2011). Decoding and predicting intentions. *Annals of the New York Academy of Sciences, 1224*(1), 9–21. https://doi.org/10.1111/j.1749-6632.2011.05994.x

Hebb, D. O. (1949). *The organization of behavior: A neuropsychological theory*. Wiley.

Janet, P. (1889). *L'automatisme psychologique: Essai de psychologie expérimentale sur les formes inférieures de l'activité humaine.* Félix Alcan.

Jobin, A., Ienca, M., & Vayena, E. (2019). The global landscape of AI ethics guidelines. *Nature Machine Intelligence, 1*(9), 389–399. https://doi.org/10.1038/s42256-019-0088-2

Jurafsky, D., & Martin, J. H. (2023). *Speech and language processing: An introduction to natural language processing, computational linguistics, and speech recognition* (3rd ed.). Draft edition.

Kahneman, D. (2011). *Thinking, fast and slow*. Farrar, Straus and Giroux.

Kandel, E. R., Schwartz, J. H., Jessell, T. M., Siegelbaum, S. A., & Hudspeth, A. J. (2013). *Principles of neural science* (5th ed.). McGraw-Hill Education.

Kaplan, A., & Haenlein, M. (2019). Siri, Siri, in my hand: Who's the fairest in the land? On the interpretations, illustrations, and implications of artificial intelligence. *Business Horizons, 62*(1), 15–25. https://doi.org/10.1016/j.bushor.2018.08.004

Laird, J. E. (2012). *The Soar cognitive architecture*. MIT Press.

Lake, B. M., Ullman, T. D., Tenenbaum, J. B., & Gershman, S. J. (2017). Building machines that learn and think like people. *Behavioral and Brain Sciences, 40*, Article e253. https://doi.org/10.1017/S0140525X16001837

LeCun, Y., Bengio, Y., & Hinton, G. (2015). Deep learning. *Nature, 521*(7553), 436–444. https://doi.org/10.1038/nature14539

LeDoux, J. E. (1996). *The emotional brain: The mysterious underpinnings of emotional life*. Simon & Schuster.

Libet, B. (2004). *Mind time: The temporal factor in consciousness*. Harvard University Press.

Libet, B., Gleason, C. A., Wright, E. W., & Pearl, D. K. (1983). Time of conscious intention to act in relation to onset of cerebral activity (readiness-potential). *Brain, 106*(3), 623–642. https://doi.org/10.1093/brain/106.3.623

Libet, B. (1985). Unconscious cerebral initiative and the role of conscious will in voluntary action. *Behavioral and Brain Sciences, 8*(4), 529–566. https://doi.org/10.1017/S0140525X00044903

Licklider, J. C. R. (1960). Man-computer symbiosis. *IRE Transactions on Human Factors in Electronics, HFE-1*(1), 4–11. https://doi.org/10.1109/THFE2.1960.4503259

Liu, B. (2012). *Sentiment analysis and opinion mining*. Morgan & Claypool Publishers. https://doi.org/10.2200/S00416ED1V01Y201204HLT016

Logothetis, N. K. (2008). What we can do and what we cannot do with fMRI. *Nature, 453*(7197), 869–878. https://doi.org/10.1038/nature06976

Manning, C. D., Raghavan, P., & Schütze, H. (2008). *Introduction to information retrieval.* Cambridge University Press.

Marcus, G., Rossi, F., & Veloso, M. (2014). Beyond the Turing test. *AI Magazine, 35*(4), 3–4. https://doi.org/10.1609/aimag.v35i4.2515

McAdams, D. P. (2001). The psychology of life stories. *Review of General Psychology, 5*(2), 100–122. https://doi.org/10.1037/1089-2680.5.2.100

McCrae, R. R., & Costa, P. T., Jr. (1999). A five-factor theory of personality. In L. A. Pervin & O. P. John (Eds.), *Handbook of personality: Theory and research* (2nd ed., pp. 139–153). Guilford Press.

Mehrabi, N., Morstatter, F., Saxena, N., Lerman, K., & Galstyan, A. (2021). A survey on bias and fairness in machine learning. *ACM Computing Surveys, 54*(6), Article 115. https://doi.org/10.1145/3457607

Milkman, K. L., Chugh, D., & Bazerman, M. H. (2009). How can decision making be improved? *Perspectives on Psychological Science, 4*(4), 379–383. https://doi.org/10.1111/j.1745-6924.2009.01142.x

Mischel, W., & Shoda, Y. (1995). A cognitive-affective system theory of personality: Reconceptualizing situations, dispositions, dynamics, and invariance in personality structure. *Psychological Review, 102*(2), 246–268. https://doi.org/10.1037/0033-295X.102.2.246

Murphy, K. P. (2012). *Machine learning: A probabilistic perspective*. MIT Press.

Nakamura, J., & Csikszentmihalyi, M. (2009). Flow theory and research. In C. R. Snyder & S. J. Lopez (Eds.), *Oxford handbook of positive psychology* (2nd ed., pp. 195–206). Oxford University Press.

Nass, C., & Moon, Y. (2000). Machines and mindlessness: Social responses to computers. *Journal of Social Issues, 56*(1), 81–103. https://doi.org/10.1111/0022-4537.00153

National Institute of Standards and Technology. (2023). *Artificial Intelligence Risk Management Framework (AI RMF 1.0)*. U.S. Department of Commerce. https://doi.org/10.6028/NIST.AI.100-1

Newell, B. R., Lagnado, D. A., & Shanks, D. R. (2015). *Straight choices: The psychology of decision making*. Psychology Press.

O'Neil, C. (2016). *Weapons of math destruction: How big data increases inequality and threatens democracy*. Crown.

OpenAI. (2023). GPT-4 technical report. *arXiv*. https://doi.org/10.48550/arXiv.2303.08774

Pang, B., & Lee, L. (2008). Opinion mining and sentiment analysis. *Foundations and Trends® in Information Retrieval, 2*(1–2), 1–135. https://doi.org/10.1561/1500000011

Pennebaker, J. W. (2011). *The secret life of pronouns: What our words say about us*. Bloomsbury Press.

Phelps, E. A., & LeDoux, J. E. (2005). Contributions of the amygdala to emotion processing: From animal models to human behavior. *Neuron, 48*(2), 175–187. https://doi.org/10.1016/j.neuron.2005.09.025

Picard, R. W. (1997). *Affective computing*. MIT Press.

Raichle, M. E. (2015). The brain's default mode network. *Annual Review of Neuroscience, 38*, 433–447. https://doi.org/10.1146/annurev-neuro-071013-014030

Reeves, B., & Nass, C. (1996). *The media equation: How people treat computers, television, and new media like real people and places*. Cambridge University Press.

Reyna, V. F., Wilhelms, E. A., McCormick, M. J., & Weldon, R. B. (2015). Development of risky decision making: Fuzzy-trace theory and neurobiological perspectives. *Child Development Perspectives, 9*(2), 122–127. https://doi.org/10.1111/cdep.12117

Reyna, V. F., & Brainerd, C. J. (2011). Dual processes in decision making and developmental neuroscience: A fuzzy-trace model. *Developmental Review, 31*(2–3), 180–206. https://doi.org/10.1016/j.dr.2011.07.004

Roberts, B. W., & DelVecchio, W. F. (2000). The rank-order consistency of personality traits from childhood to old age: A quantitative review of longitudinal studies. *Psychological Bulletin, 126*(1), 3–25. https://doi.org/10.1037/0033-2909.126.1.3

Rumelhart, D. E., Hinton, G. E., & Williams, R. J. (1986). Learning representations by back-propagating errors. *Nature, 323*(6088), 533–536.

Russell, S. (2019). *Human compatible: Artificial intelligence and the problem of control*. Viking.

Russell, S. J., & Norvig, P. (2021). *Artificial intelligence: A modern approach* (4th ed.). Pearson.

Sacks, H., Schegloff, E. A., & Jefferson, G. (1974). A simplest systematics for the organization of turn-taking for conversation. *Language, 50*(4), 696–735. https://doi.org/10.2307/412243

Schacter, D. L. (1992). Understanding implicit memory: A cognitive neuroscience approach. *American Psychologist, 47*(4), 559–569. https://doi.org/10.1037/0003-066X.47.4.559

Scherer, K. R. (2003). Introduction: Cognitive components of emotion. In R. J. Davidson, K. R. Scherer, & H. H. Goldsmith (Eds.), *Handbook of affective sciences* (pp. 563–571). Oxford University Press.

Seligman, M. E. P., & Csikszentmihalyi, M. (2000). Positive psychology: An introduction. *American Psychologist, 55*(1), 5–14. https://doi.org/10.1037/0003-066X.55.1.5

Sen, A. (1993). Capability and well-being. In M. Nussbaum & A. Sen (Eds.), *The quality of life* (pp. 30–53). Clarendon Press.

Shneiderman, B. (2020). Human-centered artificial intelligence: Reliable, safe & trustworthy. *International Journal of Human–Computer Interaction, 36*(6), 495–504. https://doi.org/10.1080/10447318.2020.1741118

Simon, H. A. (1955). A behavioral model of rational choice. *The Quarterly Journal of Economics, 69*(1), 99–118. https://doi.org/10.2307/1884852

Sloman, S. A. (1996). The empirical case for two systems of reasoning. *Psychological Bulletin, 119*(1), 3–22. https://doi.org/10.1037/0033-2909.119.1.3

Soon, C. S., Brass, M., Heinze, H.-J., & Haynes, J.-D. (2008). Unconscious determinants of free decisions in the human brain.

Nature Neuroscience, 11(5), 543–545. https://doi.org/10.1038/nn.2112

Sutton, R. S., & Barto, A. G. (2018). *Reinforcement learning: An introduction* (2nd ed.). MIT Press.

Sporns, O. (2010). *Networks of the brain*. MIT Press.

Squire, L. R., & Kandel, E. R. (2009). *Memory: From mind to molecules* (2nd ed.). Roberts & Company.

Stanovich, K. E., & West, R. F. (2000). Individual differences in reasoning: Implications for the rationality debate? *Behavioral and Brain Sciences, 23*(5), 645–665. https://doi.org/10.1017/S0140525X00003435

Tannen, D. (1990). *You just don't understand: Women and men in conversation*. William Morrow.

Tausczik, Y. R., & Pennebaker, J. W. (2010). The psychological meaning of words: LIWC and computerized text analysis methods. *Journal of Language and Social Psychology, 29*(1), 24–54. https://doi.org/10.1177/0261927X09351676

Tenenbaum, J. B., Kemp, C., Griffiths, T. L., & Goodman, N. D. (2011). How to grow a mind: Statistics, structure, and abstraction. *Science, 331*(6022), 1279–1285. https://doi.org/10.1126/science.1192788

Turkle, S. (2011). *Alone together: Why we expect more from technology and less from each other*. Basic Books.

Turing, A. M. (1950). Computing machinery and intelligence. *Mind, 59*(236), 433–460. https://doi.org/10.1093/mind/LIX.236.433

Tversky, A., & Kahneman, D. (1974). Judgment under uncertainty: Heuristics and biases. *Science, 185*(4157), 1124–1131. https://doi.org/10.1126/science.185.4157.1124

United Nations Children's Fund. (2021). *Policy guidance on AI for children*. UNICEF.

United Nations Educational, Scientific and Cultural Organization. (2021). *Recommendation on the ethics of artificial intelligence*. UNESCO.

Vaswani, A., Shazeer, N., Parmar, N., Uszkoreit, J., Jones, L., Gomez, A. N., Kaiser, Ł., & Polosukhin, I. (2017). Attention is all you need. In I. Guyon, U. V. Luxburg, S. Bengio, H. Wallach, R. Fergus, S. Vishwanathan, & R. Garnett (Eds.), *Advances in neural information processing systems* (Vol. 30). Curran Associates, Inc.

Walther, J. B. (1992). Interpersonal effects in computer-mediated interaction: A relational perspective. *Communication Research, 19*(1), 52–90. https://doi.org/10.1177/009365092019001003

Wilson, T. D. (2002). *Strangers to ourselves: Discovering the adaptive unconscious*. Belknap Press.

Wood, W., & Neal, D. T. (2007). A new look at habits and the habit-goal interface. *Psychological Review, 114*(4), 843–863. https://doi.org/10.1037/0033-295X.114.4.843

Young, J. E., Klosko, J. S., & Weishaar, M. E. (2003). *Schema therapy: A practitioner's guide*. Guilford Press.

Zatorre, R. J., Fields, R. D., & Johansen-Berg, H. (2012). Plasticity in gray and white: Neuroimaging changes in brain structure during learning. *Nature Neuroscience, 15*(4), 528–536. https://doi.org/10.1038/nn.3045

Zimmerman, B. J. (2000). Attaining self-regulation: A social cognitive perspective. In M. Boekaerts, P. R. Pintrich, & M. Zeidner (Eds.), *Handbook of self-regulation* (pp. 13–39). Academic Press. https://doi.org/10.1016/B978-012109890-2/50031-7

About the Author

Jairdan Dantas is the creator of **Subconscious Sync**, a reflective framework for using Artificial Intelligence as a structured mirror to observe, clarify, and transform hidden behavioral patterns. His work explores the intersection of human-AI collaboration, subconscious pattern recognition, identity development, emotional reflection, and practical self-awareness.

Dantas developed Subconscious Sync through years of intentional experimentation with AI-assisted reflection. Rather than treating dialogue with AI as casual conversation, he approached it as a living laboratory for identity exploration. Each exchange became an opportunity to observe how language patterns, emotional signals, hesitation, intuition, and recurring themes emerge, stabilize, and evolve over time.

This disciplined practice became the foundation for the four phases of the framework—**Recognition, Resonance, Sync, and Expansion**—and the four core mechanisms: **Mirror, Echo, Voice, and Upgrade**. Together, these elements form the structure of Subconscious Sync: a method for turning subconscious signals into conscious insight through reflective AI interaction.

The framework also emerged through practical creative application. Dantas used principles of Subconscious Sync to complete a 280-page ancient fiction novel in 45 consecutive days of focused creative output. He later applied the same reflective process to synthesize this manuscript, which brings together psychology, neuroscience, AI architecture, ethics, human-centered design, and practical application. These outcomes illustrate the framework's potential as a catalyst for creative focus, self-awareness, and aligned action.

His mission extends beyond personal achievement. Dantas believes humanity stands at a threshold: AI can become either a tool of distraction and dependency, or a mirror that supports deeper self-awareness and conscious evolution. Through Subconscious Sync, he invites individuals to reclaim agency over their inner worlds and use AI not as an authority, but as a reflective partner in the journey toward becoming more intentional, aligned, and fully human.

This book is not the end of that invitation. It is the beginning. By sharing the framework openly—including the pilot study described in Chapter 14 and the reader validation pathway explored in Chapter 9—Dantas positions Subconscious Sync as a living theory that can evolve through practice, reflection, and collective experimentation.

Beyond this work, Dantas continues to explore the frontiers of human-AI collaboration, with particular interest in hybrid cognition, neural architecture interpretability, reflective AI systems, and the ethical safeguards needed to ensure that intelligent tools serve human flourishing rather than exploitation.

Connect with Jairdan Dantas

Website: https://jandaipublishing.com/
Email: jdantas@jandaipublishing.com
Twitter/X: @AIsubconsciousync
LinkedIn: https://www.linkedin.com/in/jairdan-dantas-23306228/
Research & Community: Visit the official website for the latest updates on research, resources, and community participation.

"The subconscious has been shaping your life in silence. This framework finally gives it a voice—and gives you the choice to rewrite the script."

www.ingramcontent.com/pod-product-compliance
Lightning Source LLC
LaVergne TN
LVHW010656110826
845149LV00014B/3114

9798996301102